Restoring Grandfather Clocks

Restoring Grandfather Clocks

Eric and Brian Smith

N.A.G. Press
an imprint of Robert Hale · London

ISBN 0 7198 0270 9

Robert Hale Limited
Clerkenwell House
Clerkenwell Green
London EC1R 0HT

4 6 8 10 9 7 5 3

Photoset in North Wales by
Derek Doyle & Associates, Mold, Clwyd.
Printed in Great Britain by
St Edmundsbury Press Ltd, Bury St Edmunds, Suffolk.

Contents

6   Contents

Part IV – Variations

List of Illustrations

Introduction

This book suggests how you may restore an old grandfather clock to work reliably and to present a correct and pleasing appearance. It assumes you have inherited or otherwise come by such a clock, which is in doubtful condition, and that you are strongly drawn to improve matters. It also assumes that you have little or no practical experience of working on clocks. You will need to supplement normal household tools with some others, but to a considerable extent how far you go in this direction is up to you. Much can be done without special tools; on the other hand, it can often be done better and more easily with them. At the end of the book there is a list of firms from whom you can obtain tools and materials.

The examples illustrated in this book are fairly humble, everyday clocks such as anyone might buy or inherit without specialized or investment interest. There are two reasons for this choice. First, most grandfather clocks are in this bracket. Second, there is a point – which we should not care to define – where the risk of damage caused by a novice's intervention in antique clocks increases, as it were, exponentially. Authenticity, artistry, and money are at stake, and what is done may not be easily reversible. So consider the value of the clock (in all senses) and consider your limitations. There can be no rule, but sometimes it may be better to put the work, or at least some of it, in specialist hands.

Although the book centres on two 'case studies', which are representative of very common types of clock, it may be that the one which you propose to restore differs substantially in important respects. We have tried therefore to cover and illustrate a much wider field in a special more wide-ranging section on variations, and we hope that in this way most amateur needs will be met.

We have taken a joint interest in the book, but the parts about movements and dials were written mainly by Eric Smith, and the part about cases mainly by Brian Smith. We are indebted to so many people that it is hardly possible to name them individually, except that special thanks are due to Rita Shenton for her encouragement of the project, and to J & K Dial Restorers (of Kidlington, Oxford), who restored the dial of the clock by William Scott. But perhaps our biggest debt is to the many customers who have, often unwittingly, enlarged our experience and given

the book a field of reference much larger than the two examples round
which it moves.

Part I Overview

1   Grandfather Clocks: A Profile

Historical Perspective

As you may know, 'grandfather clock' is not a name normally used by the trade, who instead refer to 'longcase clocks'. In earlier days these clocks were also known as 'coffin clocks', for obvious reasons. The 'grandfather' label dates back to a popular American song from the middle of the nineteenth century. Whether you refer to 'longcases' or 'grandfathers' tends to depend on the sophistication of the person you are addressing. We shall refer only to 'longcase' clocks from now on.

The longcase dates from soon after the middle of the seventeenth century. Hitherto, for some sixty years, the most common domestic clock had been the wall 'lantern clock' (and it must be remembered that at this time relatively few households boasted clocks at all). Although its exact origin has been much debated, it is safe to say that the longcase originated as a screen and protection for the weights of wall clocks, such as lantern clocks. But from such a humble beginning it rapidly became a totally new piece of furniture, to whose proportions and finish the highest craftsmanship was applied. For perhaps fifty years the longcase clock was the central interest of clockmakers and casemakers in London. Then, although the longcase was not abandoned, the focus shifted more towards equally fine smaller bracket clocks, the second clock of a wealthy household. Meanwhile, the fame of the longcase spread outwards from London and longcases were the principal output of clockmakers and casemakers up and down the country. Thus there was major production of this type of clock for some two hundred years, and thereafter longcases have continued to be made, though no longer in the mainstream.

Mention has been made of 'clockmakers and casemakers'. These two crafts were, from the first, distinct, although some country clockmakers probably made their own cases. Dials also were a separate industry and in fact it is very difficult to generalize throughout the longcase period as to just how much work was done by the maker, whose name is normally written on the dial. Certainly by late in the eighteenth century whole movements could be bought from specialist houses and dials from others, although even then you often find that the wheels just behind the dial

15

('motion wheels') and levers of the striking mechanism are of a different quality and made locally. Sometimes you find the name of a London maker stamped on the movement of a provincial dial – particularly after about 1830, when railway transport made an impact.

Hence, although the principal reason for a dial and movement not 'belonging' to each other is that someone later has for commercial reasons 'married' them, the increasing batch production of parts of the clock in different locations can result in apparent anomalies which are quite 'genuine' (for example, a shaft ('arbor') being provided for a seconds hand but no seconds hand indication on the dial). Arrangements were also made so that a dial not produced for a particular movement could be quickly and easily fitted to it. Well-built cases to many specified designs could be ordered. Nonetheless, for practical purposes (particularly for defining date and place of origin), the name on the dial is taken to be that of the proprietor clockmaker, the business responsible for clock and case. (Casemakers are hardly ever named anywhere on a clock.)

There is a good chance that you can discover the approximate date and locality of your clock from reference to the classic list *Watchmakers and Clockmakers of the World* by G.H. Baillie, with the second volume by Brian Loomes. This is available in most public libraries. There are subsidiary and localized lists in many of the books on longcase clocks, some of which are listed at the end of this book. Throughout the period there are, for reasons which can only be conjectured, clocks which are unsigned, and then dating them is a matter of assessing styles of workmanship. Book illustrations may be helpful in this respect (see Select Further Reading – Historical and Reference section). In all work on provenance it is essential to be most wary; very frequently the movement, dial and case of a longcase clock have not always been together, and the clock for various reasons is a hybrid. That need not produce an unattractive clock or stop you from enjoying it, but it does, of course, reduce monetary value and it may well confuse the identifying of date and place. In the books about longcase clocks there are hints on how to detect fraud (now or in the past), but if you suspect your clock is not entirely 'right' (as dealers tend to say) it may well be worth seeking professional advice; the major London auction houses are often very helpful, at no or small cost.

Scope and Variations

Over such a long period, and over such a large geographical area (that is, the British Isles) with slow communication, there is, naturally, no single prototype, and indeed this is often a help in dating. It does, however, also mean that the clock which you wish to restore may differ significantly from examples discussed here. For this reason, some of the main variations which are found are described separately. Other types of casework and

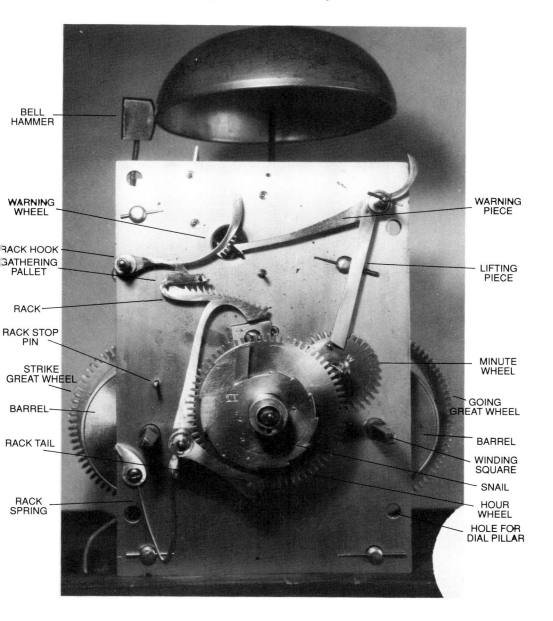

Fig. 1   Eight-day movement (front)

mechanism – and particularly more elaborate forms of striking, chiming and musical-work – will be discussed and, in many instances, illustrated in the books which appear in the list of further reading. Caution (that is to say, probably specialist advice) is indicated where your clock has more than one bell, or where its dial indications are other than the time plus day-of-the month aperture (or dial) and moon-phases – these last two being optional extras which may not be present. Twentieth century (including spring-driven) clocks also are outside the scope of this book.

The Two Types

Within this large variety there is a major division of types – the thirty-hour and the eight-day. These were, from the start, distinct. The thirty-hour clock is not a cheap and late development. You can identify the two types by whether or not the clock is wound with a key.

Eight-day clocks are wound by keys passed through holes in the dial and therefore almost always have hinged doors in their tops ('hoods'). With the exception of a type of striking known as 'internal countwheel', which is discussed later, their movements soon evolved into a standard design, shown in Fig. 1.

Thirty-hour clocks are wound by pulling down a weight in the body ('trunk') of the case and have no winding keys or key-holes. They have, of course, to be wound every day. As access to the dial is needed only for setting the hands, the hoods may not have opening doors, the dial being reached by sliding the hood forward. At first, however, hoods were raised upwards clear of the dials. Occasional traces of these vertical slides are still found.

In general, thirty-hour clocks are (and always were) simpler and cheaper than eight-day clocks, although they may be capable of just as good time-keeping. There are two distinct types of thirty-hour movement – the posted (or 'birdcage') and the plated. The difference is, on the whole, due to locality rather than date; although the posted movement may seem to look older and cruder, such clocks were in fact made into the nineteenth century, while some of the oldest known thirty-hour clocks have the plated structure. The posted design derived directly from the lantern clock, while the origins of the plated type are more complex. Typical layouts of both types (where there tends to be more variation than in eight-day clocks) are shown in Figs. 2–4.

The earliest longcase clocks had only an hour hand and dials divided into quarters rather than minutes. Eight-day clocks rapidly moved into showing minutes, but single-handed thirty-hour clocks were made throughout the eighteenth century. Thus posted or plated movements may have one hand or two hands with different train arrangements – within the basic divisions there are many combinations. We shall be looking at a plated two-handed

BELL STANDARD

BELL HAMMER

LIFTING/WARNING PIECE

GOING GREAT WHEEL

MINUTE WHEEL

HOUR WHEEL

STRIKING GREAT WHEEL

SEATBOARD

Fig. 2   Thirty-hour plated movement (front)

clock in detail, but the variations are outlined for reference in Part IV.

Over the years, the thirty-hour clock has tended to suffer as a 'poor relation'. The enormous range and variety of these clocks has never been extensively discussed. It may reasonably be held that they are often undervalued, and revaluation might follow on the full-length study which has yet to be made. There is no reason to belittle your clock because it happens to be of thirty-hour rather than eight-day duration, or if it has (whether thirty-hour or eight-day) a 'painted dial' rather than a dial of silvered brass. (A painted dial is also known as a 'white dial'.) Apart from the fact that painted dials were not made before 1770, and so a clock with such a dial is not of the earliest, these different dials should be assessed on

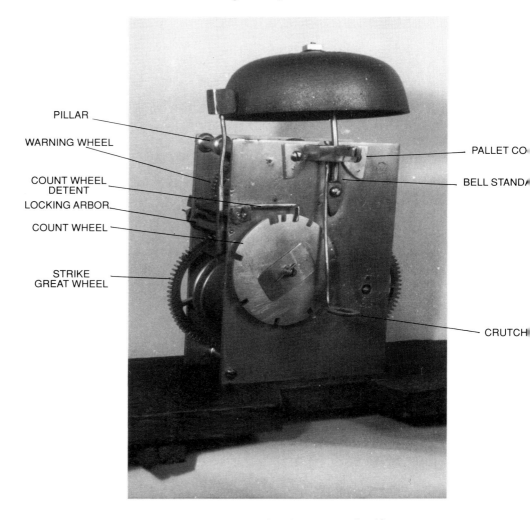

PILLAR

WARNING WHEEL

COUNT WHEEL
DETENT

LOCKING ARBOR

COUNT WHEEL

STRIKE
GREAT WHEEL

PALLET CO

BELL STAND

CRUTCH

Fig. 3   Thirty-hour plated movement (back)

their own merits. Remember also that a brass dial is more likely to be unoriginal (because for decades brass dials were preferred to painted and many exchanges or 'marriages' were made).

It is worth considering one obvious thing when looking at clocks from the late eighteenth or early nineteenth centuries, because with respect to it thirty-hour and eight-day clocks differ significantly. Painted dials were fitted direct to thirty-hour movements, but in nearly all eight-day movements with these dials the dial was fitted with an intervening cast iron 'falseplate'. This was introduced by the dialmakers in the 1770s to facilitate

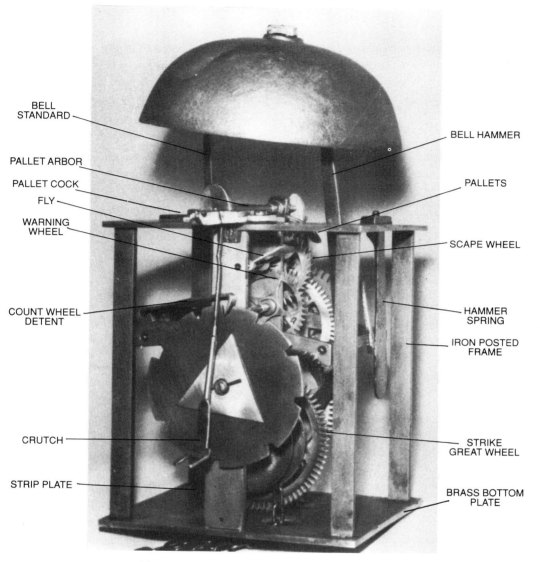

BELL
STANDARD

PALLET ARBOR

PALLET COCK

FLY

WARNING
WHEEL

COUNT WHEEL
DETENT

CRUTCH

STRIP PLATE

BELL HAMMER

PALLETS

SCAPE WHEEL

HAMMER
SPRING

IRON POSTED
FRAME

STRIKE
GREAT WHEEL

BRASS BOTTOM
PLATE

Fig. 4   Thirty-hour posted movement (back)

fitting a dial not made on the spot and having the complication of winding holes. It is what we now might term an 'adaptor' and was almost invariably used, so its presence, absence or alteration may suggest something of the history of the clock. As the device was not used with brass dials, its presence with a brass dial strongly suggests that the dial has been changed.

2 Principles and Examples

How the Clock Works

Skip this section if you are familiar with clockworks. The names of the main movement parts are given in Figs. 1–4, which can be used for reference.

The longcase clock consists of two weight-driven motors, either side by side in their frame or going from front to back. One motor is concerned with telling the time – the 'going train' – and one with striking the hour – the 'striking train'.

Both motors are interrupted in their running, the going side being held, second by second, by a device known as the 'escapement', and the striking side by a locking arrangement which is released once an hour by the going. The escapement consists of a wheel with ratchet teeth and two arms (pallets) which engage with them. Each train is driven by a weight attached to a line or chain and passing round a cylinder ('barrel') or pulley attached to a large wheel (the 'greatwheel'). By ingenious arrangement of the lines, however, the thirty-hour clock has only one weight for the two trains.

It is most important to recognize that the pendulum in no way drives the going side, but merely causes the interruption of its motion once a second via the escapement. The timekeeping is controlled by the length (not the weight or mass) of the pendulum; it is virtually independent of the power applied or how heavy the pendulum 'bob' may be. However, the heavier the pendulum bob, the more control it exercises on the going side and the more *regular* the time-keeping should be.

After the greatwheel, the power from the weight passes through a train of gearwheels and pinions (the latter being small, usually steel, solid wheels). This is carefully calculated so that, for the going, the hands revolve once an hour (and once in twelve hours), and the weight takes either thirty hours or eight days to fall to the bottom of the case. For the striking, released by the going, it is ensured again that the weight will not reach the case bottom before the required duration has elapsed. Where there are two weights, they descend roughly parallel, but when the clock is striking high-number hours (say from 8.00 to 12.00), the striking weight falls further at each release and will be found out of step in the case with the going weight.

It is not necessary for you to know in detail the theory of gearing or to get involved in counting the teeth on gearwheels, unless a wheel should be missing or damaged beyond repair. The calculations then needed are explained later. Bear in mind that it is the relationship of the diameters of two meshing wheels which is critical, and this is embodied in the number of teeth which each has.

You will probably recognize that the missing item in this account is how to keep the pendulum swinging. Without a push now and again it would come to a stop fairly quickly, since it is connected to the going by the 'crutch', the long wire arm descending from the pallets, which creates friction. The pendulum's swing ('vibration') is in fact kept up by the escapement, which is so designed that it administers a little push ('impulse') at each swing. It maintains a virtually constant amplitude ('arc of vibration') but, in any case, the vital property of a pendulum is isochronism – it takes almost exactly the same time to make a big swing as to make a small one. This is why its adoption in preference to other controllers in the late seventeenth century, when the longcase clock first appeared, was such a major step forward; previously the power applied, inevitably variable for many reasons, greatly influenced the regularity of the time-keeping, and indeed regulation was principally by varying the weight used.

This book centres on the restoration of a 'typical' clock, represented by specific thirty-hour and eight-day examples, and a description of these two may be helpful. Of course there is no such thing as a typical longcase clock, but these examples are of very common types.

The Thirty-hour Clock (Fig. 5)

The dial of the thirty-hour clock in Figure 5 is printed with 'G. Burgess, Bridport' – although, because it is in only moderate condition, this is not immediately obvious (Fig. 6). The maker or retailer is not listed in Baillie's *Watchmakers and Clockmakers of the World*, or its supplement by Brian Loomes, but it is noted by T. Tribe and P. Whatmoor (*Dorset Clocks and Clockmakers*, p. 72) that Burgess had a shop in Bridport High Street in 1850. The dial was certainly bought in, and it is likely that the movement was also. Burgess would probably arrange the casing and perhaps the assembly and finishing work. Country clock-making tends to be conservative and, by impression, one might have dated this before 1850. Regardless of its exact date, it is late in the history of the thirty-hour clock.

Dial, movement and case appear to 'belong' to each other, but the hands, though plausible in style, are too heavy and seem to be individually-made replacements. This is a sound Dorset clock from the early nineteenth century, showing the effects of time, but little repaired or altered. The case is made of solid oak panels, the plinth cross-banded in

Fig. 6   Dial of Burgess clock

Fig. 5   Thirty-hour clock by
G. Burgess (Bridport) *c*. 1830

rosewood, with an inlaid circle of the same wood centred in the panel. In the centre of the door is a marquetry shell, the background being harewood (sycamore dyed green), and the shell being made of boxwood with shaded areas. The door is flanked by quarter corner columns set into the front edges of the case. The hood has a swan-neck pediment with a boss between the two arms bearing a brass finial. The door is of oak, veneered in cross-grained mahogany and mitred at the corners. Repairs which obviously have to be carried out include the gaping split in the front panel of the plinth, various pieces of missing veneer, and worm-holes in the base of the columns.

For what appears a simple cottage clock, this is quite an elaborate case, and the mechanism also is more than basic. The going (time) train has four wheels where three is typical of the cheaper and simpler clocks. Yet despite this, the clock has no seconds hand or day-of-the-month indicator (both usual – though by no means universal – with the longer train). Also, it has a traditional square rather than arched dial. Arched dials, often with phases of the moon, were common in the more expensive four-wheeled clocks. The striking train is on the right (from the front) and the going train on the left. This arrangement is almost invariable on thirty-hour clocks and, along with the single weight and lack of keyholes, distinguishes them from eight-day clocks, which have striking on the left. In this particular movement there are no parts obviously missing or any major defects.

The Eight-day Clock (Fig. 7)

The dial is signed 'Wm. Scott', but there is no indication of place. Movement and dial do not belong to the case, and the whole is a rescue operation whose parts are reasonably compatible and result in a pleasing clock. We are not concerned with antique values here – for practical purposes we have a movement and case, which are treated separately in this book. However, it is quite likely that your own clock will prove to be a hybrid or to have been radically altered over time. Some of the books in the list of further reading will help you to clarify the matter. Such clocks are, of course, strictly of lesser value, but they can still be enjoyed. Also, of course, they have to be repaired and restored as much as any other.

Obviously we cannot in these circumstances use the case style (in fact, probably Lancashire of the early nineteenth century) to suggest date or locality for the whole. The falseplate is unnamed but the back of the moon disc is stamped 'Wilson, Birm' – a well-known dial-making firm in the early nineteenth century. There is no reason (examples would be unused holes on falseplate or movement, holes for hands and key not lining up properly) to think that dial and movement do not belong together, and all in all they seem likely to be some fifty years earlier than the Burgess clock. Baillie lists several William Scotts, the most likely candidate being from Newcastle

Fig. 8   Dial of Scott clock

Fig. 7   Eight-day clock by Wm. Scott
(Newcastle) *c.* 1790

and working at the turn of the century, a date supported by the simple design of opposed birds on the dial (Fig. 8).

The front panel of the plinth is again of oak, but with cross-bandings of mahogany, mitred at the corners and with an ebonized inlaid line separating it from the panel. The trunk of the case has a much longer door than the Burgess, again of oak, and has a crested top, which is a Northern feature. It has been cut down, to perhaps one-third of its original thickness. The presence of a frame of bearers behind it leads one to suspect that the door was once badly warped (a common problem), the repair being effective rather than beautiful or true to modern practice. The back of the case has been replaced tidily with a sheet of hardboard; clearly the woodworm, which has severely attacked elsewhere, found the original pine back exceptionally tasty. The front of the trunk is veneered in mahogany with small inlaid lines used to define the panels above and below the canted corners. The hood is again swan-necked, but with an arched door cross-banded in mahogany. There are two slender reeded columns flanking it, with brass capitals and feet. It is an imposing case, without the excessive width which (according to taste) can mar these Northern clocks. At first sight repairs which clearly will be needed include the split in the plinth, the hood glass (apparently original but cracked badly), and replacement of a finial in the hood.

The movement has no oddities or unusual features but it shows some attention to detail and craft in, for example, the very fine spokes ('crossings') to the wheels and the pleasing curves of the steel parts on the frontplate. It looks complete, except that there is no mechanism to drive the moon-phase disc, and bell and bell standard are missing, as is the gathering pallet (a crucial part of the striking, as we shall see). Even those who have a horror of 'over-restored' dials are likely to feel that the dial will need considerable attention (Fig. 8).

Part II   Movements

3   Tools and Materials

In considering tools and materials likely to be required, one has to bear in mind a wide variety – both of clocks and of readers and their circumstances. In any list offered, not all will always be required and, equally, something necessary in some instances will probably go unmentioned.

We have distinguished tools which might be available in many homes from those which would probably need to come from specialist suppliers. Some will like to have the 'correct' tools while others, for various reasons, will prefer to exercise the amateur's privilege of improvising to some extent. It is accepted that many will try to do the best they can with whatever tools are to hand, but an indication of what would be useful, now or in future, is worthwhile.

It would be wise to look through this book and form an estimate of the work to be done in your own instance before rushing to the supplier with an order, for generally specialist tools are good quality and not cheap. On the other hand, there are jobs which cannot be skimped – such as work on pivots and plate holes – and for which nothing less than the 'real' tools (a pivot burnisher and a set of broaches) will do.

Tools and materials needed for casework are discussed in Chapter 12.

1. Tools

HOUSEHOLD

— light hammer. Preferably with ball-peen (i.e. domed) head, used for riveting.

— screwdrivers. It is difficult to have too many. A medium sized (say about 8″, 200 mm long, the blade ¼″, 5–7 mm) and smaller sized (perhaps electrician's screwdriver, blade about 3/32″, 2 mm) screwdriver are indispensable and can be sharpened as needed. A set of 'jewellers' screwdrivers' with loose tops is very useful; the index finger applies pressure to the top while the barrel is turned between finger and thumb. A 'gripping' screwdriver is handy, but in our experience magnetic screwdrivers are more nuisance than they are worth.

31

— 'junior' hacksaw. If you have a choice, a fine multi-toothed blade is most useful.

— two or three coarse and medium files, 6–8'' (150–200 mm) long. Should be bought with handles, for safety.

— general purpose and small pliers. Very-long-nosed pliers are occasionally useful for access, but generally those with shorter, pointed noses are most useful; a major use is in gripping and extracting the tightly fitted tapered pins used to assemble clock movements.

— glass-fibre rust-removing pencil brush. Available from motoring and hardware shops as well as specialist suppliers.

— small bench vice, jaws some 2'' (50 mm) across. These may be had for screwing or clamping to a bench or with suction-fitting to a smooth surface if you are using a table to work on. There are many patterns. Try to choose one with little play in the screw and where the jaws close to form a level top. If possible, avoid sharply serrated jaws, or obtain (or make) wooden or brass chops to fit over the jaws and protect material (notably brass) being held.

— hand drill with assorted drill bits from 1/32'' (1 mm) up to ¼'' (6 mm). If you have one, a powered bench drill is extremely useful, but hand-held power drills are too heavy and violent. If you are starting out, leave purchase of a drill and bits until the need arises. Generally, one is working with existing holes, and you may not need a drill.

— soldering tools. Soft (lead) solder is seldom used in clockwork because it is not strong enough and is inclined to be messy. However, you might need it for repairing pallets or a broken wheel. Paste solder, such as Easiweld, is a convenient form. There is occasional need for brazing with hard solder. If this arises, the kits available with refillable butane torches from do-it-yourself stores are normally sufficient. Restorers have to decide, on grounds such as conservation, strength and appearance, between repairing broken parts (such as clock hands) and replacing them.

— sharpening stone. A fine carborundum stone is useful for sharpening screwdrivers and for one or two jobs on the movement. A hand stone is quite sufficient.

— lighting. Although our ancestors accomplished miracles with what now seems very inadequate lighting, a good light is easier and safer. Before you start, consider where you are going to work, where to make the most of daylight (which is still best) and whether you can provide an adjustable additional light. If this can be fluorescent, or run off a low voltage, so much the better, because working with 'reading' or Anglepoise lights with standard bulbs can be very hot and wearing.

— a large plastic washing-up bowl (or similar) is needed for soaking parts in cleaning solutions. If you should have an arched brass dial, the backplate will be too big for any such tank and the plate must be completely immersed; a plastic drip tray (motoring stores) or plant tray (do-it-yourself and garden stores) are useful for this. Several small containers, from large match-box size up, will be found helpful for separating out parts not being worked on.

— a supply of rags, mainly cotton. Old underwear is ideal.

— a feeler gauge (as for adjusting car ignition points) is very useful in setting escapements. It can be metric or Imperial since it is used as a simple gauge.

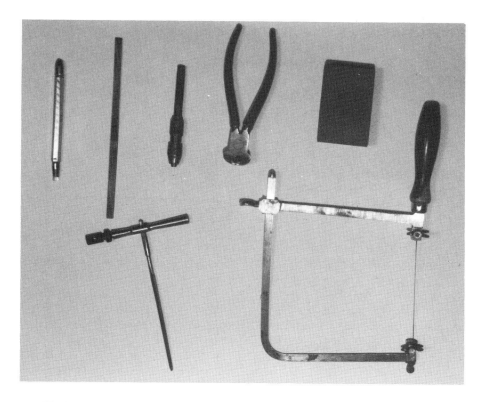

Fig. 9   Selected tools: *left to right. Top row:* glass fibre brush, pivot burnisher, pin-chuck, top-cut nippers, rubber abrasive block: *Bottom row:* tap wrench and broach, piercing saw.

SPECIALIST (FIG. 9)

In general these tools – which have been arranged in a rough order of priority – will have to be obtained from a clock materials supply house. There will be some such businesses listed in the Yellow Pages directory and some operate national mail order services with catalogues. Help can be obtained from the list of suppliers at the end of this book.

— abrasives and cleaning materials. General brass cleaning has been much simplified in recent years by the development of abrasive rubber blocks (Fig. 9), known as Garryflex and other trade names. These are not expensive and can be had in fine, medium and coarse grades. Stained and badly discoloured brass can be restored with them to a finely-grained matt finish, although care has to be taken to avoid rounding sharp square edges and to keep the light graining in a straight line. Attention also has to be given to removing all traces of the abrasive sludge which tends to follow in their wake. There is still a use for abrasive papers, however, and a supply of 'wet or dry' paper in a fine grade (400) is also needed. Using an 'impact' glue, some of this can be stuck round wooden sticks about 1″ (25 mm) wide to form useful 'buffs', or emery buffs in assorted grades can be bought. Buffs are particularly useful in cleaning and de-rusting steel. You also need brushes, or at least a brush, for cleaning. A soft brass wire brush with four rows of wires is possibly best for general use. An old or new rather soft toothbrush is also a useful accessory, as is a small brass wire brush of the kind used for cleaning suede shoes.

— top-cut nippers (Fig. 9). The wire-cutting blades which are part of many general purpose pliers are usually not sharp or accessible enough for cutting taper pins, and for this frequent job good nippers, with hardened blades, are needed. These are cut, of course, by compression; the craftsman is recognizable by the fact that he or she does not leave pins sharp-ended from the nippers but files the ends square and flat.

— tweezers. From the enormous variety available, choose some with fair strength and strong points – for a start. You need to get right inside a movement with them, so tweezers not less than 4–5″ (100–125 mm) long are preferable. To save constant annoyance, pay a little more to obtain anti-magnetic tweezers.

— set of needle files and one of the many adjustable grips to protect you from their tangs; or, preferably, wooden handles (which can be driven on with the tang brought to red heat). To begin with you need at least square, knife, flat and round files.

— pivot burnisher (Fig. 9). This is a specialized tool, one side an extremely fine file and the other ground flat steel. You may feel it is expensive for what it is, but there really is no substitute in the job of reducing friction in the gear trains to a minimum. You want a flat burnisher (not an oval one), and the ¼″ (5 mm) width is most convenient.

— pin vices (Fig. 9). These are small handled chucks for holding the ends of pins, arbors (axles) etc., which are twirled for cleaning and polishing.

— broaches, and holder – for which a tap wrench or pin vice will, however, serve (Fig. 9). The broach is used for enlarging, and slightly moving, holes. The correct tightness or freedom of a clock wheel pivot in its plate hole is a matter of feel rather than of measurement, and so it is obtained by judicious use of tapered broaches rather than by drilling. You will need an assortment, ranging from (measuring the middle of the taper) about $\frac{1}{32}$″

(1 mm) up to about ⅛'' (4 mm). The large ones are relatively expensive, so be sure that your project requires one before buying over about $\frac{1}{16}$'' (2 mm). This depends principally on how loose in its holes are the barrels or biggest wheels (greatwheels).

— punches. An enormous range of punches is made, some for highly specialized jobs. Your main need is a sharp pointed centre-punch (for accurate marking and starting of holes in metal). Do not buy a cheap one – a hardened, lasting point is required. If you can then afford it, buy a small set of assorted punches, some solid and some hollow-ended; you never know when you may need them, although for some jobs it is possible to make your own.

— eyeglass. This may be an inexpensive boost for morale, but it will not be greatly used in restoring movements as large as those of longcase clocks. In fact its main use would be for examining the condition of pivots. However, if you think you might ever do any more work on clocks, it will be a worthwhile investment. There are many types, for use with or without spectacles, and many magnifications. A lens giving 3× magnification might be most useful, and with this you will need to hold the object some 4'' (100 mm) away.

— piercing saw and blades (Fig. 9). You are unlikely to have any great call for this item unless you have to make a missing hand or hands, but then it is indispensable. If you are new to this sort of work, you will break many blades, so it is as well to buy two or three packets. There is a large range of sizes. If buying by post, go for a couple of mid-range sizes. If you can see the blades, choose a size where the gap between two blade teeth is slightly less than the thickness of the metal which you want to cut – in other words, where the metal will not quite fit between two blade teeth. It is much easier to cut with a blade on the fine side. (A blade with thirty-six teeth to the inch is a useful size). Most, if not all, piercing saw frames now available have soft blade-clamping screws which soon lose their thread; it is worth replacing them with hardened (such as hexagon socket head) screws.

2. *Materials*

HOUSEHOLD

— metal (brass) polish. Everyone discovers a favourite and we have no particular recommendation. We suggest you keep it to a simple rub-on, wipe-off cream.

— chamois leather ('washleather'). Buy real leather. There does not seem to be a satisfactory synthetic 'chammy' for metal polishing. Alternate with rags (preferably cotton) for applying polish. Cut into strips (as when making emery buffs) and stick to lengths of wood to form good buffs; a buff formed of 'chammy' round quadrant wood moulding is particularly useful.

— household ammonia (diluted) and liquid soap, the basic cleaning materials for brass. (Commercial preparations – often basically the same – are available from suppliers.) A suitable mixture is given in the next chapter.

— cream of tartar (from a grocer's/cooking store) is used in the process of silvering brass dial rings.

— acrylic paints and India ink, with an assortment of fine pens and brushes and fine (i.e. 0.1 mm) black marker pens may be obtained from art shops and used in touching up painted dials. A gold marker pen is also often useful.

— ultra-violet light. This is useful for deciphering inscriptions on painted dials. The kind of battery light used for security-marking, available from locksmiths and elsewhere, is satisfactory.

SPECIALIST

— clock oil. While there are many brands and grades of clock oil, it cannot be overstressed that *oil must be bought from a specialist house*. No other oil is suitable and some others may do actual harm. For a few pence, buy an oiler at the same time – or make one with the point of a pin flattened into an arrow and mounted in a short length of dowel.

— pegwood is used for cleaning out holes. Sharpened matchsticks are a reasonable alternative. Cocktail sticks are rather too hard.

— clock pins. Tapered pins are the main means, other than screws, of securing parts. You need steel rather than brass and it will be best to buy either a large assortment or a pack of 'universal' pins (which are of a size to be cut up for various uses).

— Loctite 601 or 641 (601 is stronger). This metal adhesive is now much used for fitting wheels and pinions to arbors in repair work. A 110 ml bottle will last a long time.

— clock bushes (for tightening and trueing plate holes). Establish a need for them in your project (see Chapter 5) before buying a suitable assortment.

— clear lacquer (shellac, not cellulose), used to protect dials and other bright surfaces such as plates. Spray lacquers usually do not produce an acceptable finish.

— blueing enamel may be used as an alternative to heat-processing in blueing steel hands (particularly where a soldered repair is to be coloured). Producing a rather better finish is gun blueing paste (from a gunsmith's).

— silvering powder for re-silvering dial rings. Special finishing powder is also sold, but household cream of tartar is as effective and cheaper.

— black engraving wax (or black sealing wax if available), for filling engraved dial characters, if necessary.

— gut or wire line, rope or chain, depending on the type of clock, and identified by the shape of pulleys (see Chapter 3).

4   Dismantling and Cleaning

Order of Work

It is general practice to carry out most repairs before cleaning the movement – cleaning immediately precedes reassembly, when everything else has been done to the movement. There are good reasons for this arrangement. The positions of many parts, present or now missing, are visible in the uncleaned state, and some of the clock's history is clear. Moreover, any marks made in making new repairs can be taken up at the time of cleaning, and this sequence involves only one dismantlement and reassembly.

Occasionally, however, a movement is so dirty that it must be given at least some sort of clean before much can be seen at all. Moreover, while the worst instances can be identified while the movement is still assembled and able to be lightly run by hand, the wear of pivots and holes is more easily seen with the movement cleaned. The amateur is happier working with cleaned surfaces and feels progress is being made. More pride can be taken in the work.

In this book, while suggesting close observation of the movement before it is dismantled (with note pad to hand!), we put cleaning at the beginning. This does, of course, mean that there may have to be some further cleaning and polishing before assembly, but time is less important than it is to the professional. Cleaning first may be more rewarding and lead to a better result in the circumstances. It means also that you become thoroughly familiar with individual parts before making any alterations. On the other hand, it *is* necessary to guard against being so entranced by the cleaned movement that you give less than full attention to repairs and servicing, which are quite as important. In this sequence, that is, when you have cleaned, your work has only just begun.

First Inspection

Carry out a preliminary inspection of your clock as it is received. First remove the weight(s) and then the pendulum; be wary with the pendulum – sometimes a movement with dial is unstable when weights and pendulum are removed and they can tip forward, with risk of damage both to themselves and to the observer. The movement is fastened to (or may just rest on) a stout piece of wood known as the 'seatboard'. Sometimes the seatboard has been screwed or nailed to the side 'cheeks' (uprights) of the case, and sometimes it just rests on them – it is in the latter case that there is some risk of it falling. The fastening is most often (as in the Burgess clock) by screwed hooks round the pillars. Less frequently, screws are passed through the seatboard into the pillar. This latter is the earlier method and tends to be found on better quality movements right through the longcase period (it is used in the Scott clock).

Remove the hands (or single hand) and dial. The minute hand is usually fitted with a tapered pin. The fitting of hour hands varies but should be clear from observation. Both the example clocks use the commonest method – the hand is pressed onto the pipe and located by a small screw. Quite often, however, the bosses of hour hands are squared, when they may be just a press fit or may be pinned across the corners. The dials are most often held by three or four thick pins, but those of posted thirty-hour movements are hooked on at the top.

In your first inspection, try to assess what, if anything, is severely damaged or missing. Compare your movement with those in Figs. 1–4 – it will differ in details but the essentials will be similar. With your finger try to revolve both greatwheels (the bottom wheels, with pulleys or barrels attached). What you want to see is a corresponding movement at the top of each train – the strike fly and the scapewheel. This assures you that no wheels are missing from the train. The pallets should embrace the scapewheel, which has ratchet-shaped teeth. The crutch descends from the back bracket ('pallet cock') to the pendulum; pressure on going train wheels should produce at least a movement of the pallets and may, if you adjust the level at which you are holding the movement, lead to definite ticking, the pallets and crutch swinging from side to side. This indicates that there is nothing radically wrong with the escapement, the heart of the clock. Both of the example clocks responded positively here, though neither had kept going in its case for any period.

On the thirty-hour striking side, lift the countwheel detent out of the slot on the countwheel (attached to the backplate), again apply pressure to the train, and observe how the bell hammer is operated by pins on the great wheel. Notice also how the train is locked after striking – this will *not* be (as superficially appears) by the falling of the countwheel detent into a countwheel slot; that action only determines the time when the train is actually locked elsewhere in the movement. The locking in a thirty-hour clock is most often by the catching of another hook or detent on the broken rim of the wheel next to the greatwheel (the 'hoopwheel'). On the eight-day clock, press on the strike greatwheel and raise the rackhook. The rack should fall and the train be free to raise it up again, when a tailed

Fig. 10   Burgess movement before
cleaning (front)

Fig. 11   Burgess movement before
cleaning (back)

tooth on an extended wheel arbor (the 'gathering pallet' on the 'locking wheel') catches on a pin in the rack to hold it locked.

Figs. 10 and 11 show the Burgess movement before cleaning. To the left of the front will be seen a brass bracket supporting the greatwheel arbor, which is normally pivoted straight into the plate. There is a similar slab inside the backplate; together they move the wheel forward and at this stage arouse suspicion that either damage to the meshing pinion or the total break-up of the original plate holes called for this drastic repair. They are shown more clearly in Fig. 12, while Fig. 13 shows a damaged striking wheel. It is worth assessing the condition of the pinions and pivots, both potential sites for serious wear, at this stage. Here there was wear, but no really deep hollows, on the faster pinions, while nearly all the holes had been closed up by blows from a punch, and some had been bushed. (These repairs are discussed in the next chapter.) Nonetheless, a number of pivots were extremely loose in their holes, and this of course meant that the gears were not properly located and could not run smoothly. Fig. 14 shows from the back the sorry state of the plates and holes.

After this inspection, the seatboard was removed, washed and scrubbed.

Fig. 12   Reinforcements of greatwheel holes

Fig. 13   Damaged warning wheel

Fig. 14   Distressed backplate

In this case the clearance holes had been made, as is not uncommon, into a single wide slot for the chains (Fig. 15), but often there are separate holes and the chain or rope must be broken, rather than simply pulled through, to remove the board.

Fig. 15   Seatboard cutouts

The Scott movement was similarly checked over, the main discovery being that there was no arrangement for driving the moonwork in the dial arch, although a stud (which would be part of it) protruded from the back of the dial. Another serious defect was that there was no pallet for gathering up the striking rack. The gearwork was not extensively worn; nor, at first sight, were the pivots. However, it later became clear that these were mostly abnormally fine and the holes had been tightened round them over the years by repairers, some of whose work had to be made good. On an eight-day clock, the lines pass twice through the seatboard and must be undone or removed before it can be freed. Generally they should be replaced with new, and so can simply be cut away at this stage. Fig. 16 shows the Scott clock as inspected, while the falseplate is seen in Fig. 17. The falseplate has large holes to receive the dial pillars, and then four pillars of its own which are pinned to the movement. Sections are cut out to clear parts protruding from the frontplate. However, there may not be any such parts – the cut-outs were standard. Treatment with the wire brush is usually sufficient for falseplates.

Fig. 16   Scott movement before cleaning   Fig. 17   Scott falseplate

Dismantling

Proceeding from the back to the front, take off all the external movement parts. These consist broadly of the pallet cock and pallets, countwheel if any, motion wheels (external wheels in front, gearing the hands and indicators to the movement) and several components of the striking work which are on the front plate of the eight-day movement. Some of these parts are fixed to the plates with screws, and here note that screws on longcase clocks, depending partly on date, are often not interchangeable. It is as well, therefore, to store them labelled while work progresses. A good way to do this is to use an inverted cardboard box or tin, dropping the screw shanks through punched holes. As dismantling goes forward, you will find other peculiarities worth noting. For example, the bell standard of the Burgess clock was found to be riveted to the plate instead of screwed and was left intact, while the countwheel mounting-stud on the backplate was found to be very loose (a common fault in striking). The many pins are best discarded to replace with new. If the wheel to which the minute hand is attached (the 'cannon pinion') presses against a bowed spring on the front plate, notice the position of this spring – it should present its convex face to the plate.

Next remove the tapered pins from the pillars which hold the plates together, and raise the front plate. These pins sometimes have to be driven out with a punch or even drilled out. Lift the frontplate carefully, trying to ensure that everything between plates remains located on the backplate so that you can study, and if necessary draw diagrams of, the arrangement. With practice you will have no difficulty in identifying loose parts, but for the moment keep all the going wheels and all the striking wheels together – the simplest plan is to link each group with soft wire, and this will be useful when it comes to cleaning. In a thirty-hour clock the going wheels are on the left and centre, while in the eight-day movement they are on the right and centre. There is no difficulty in distinguishing the two thirty-hour greatwheels, since only the striking greatwheel carries a winding ratchet; but it is as well to mark with punched dots the eight-day striking greatwheel. Both eight-day greatwheels have ratchets and they are not interchangeable. Here you may find scratches from previous ventures – 'W' means 'watch' (the old term for 'going') and 'S', of course, means 'striking'. Note, and if necessary sketch, the arrangement of steel striking arbors on the extreme right of the thirty-hour movement.

Brass and steel parts are cleaned in different ways, so separate the metals. Some parts contain both metals (the wheel assemblies, for instance), and in these the brass should be cleaned first.

Cleaning the Brass

The cleaning of movements by a simple 'dunking' in paraffin or petrol should be discouraged. Although that would take care of one object in cleaning – the need for the mechanism to be cleared of gross dirt and old congealed oil – it would be inadequate and would do little for the clock's appearance. Nowadays, although a high polish is not usual (or, as a rule, true to the original finish), cleaning must entail complete dismantlement and the restoration of the metals' surface appearance. In the course of this cleaning, moreover, will appear the need for many repairs not otherwise evident. Traditional more thorough methods of cleaning were that of the 'grease brush' – repeated brushing of the parts with metal polish and finishing with chalk – and the 'soak' – leaving the parts in a special solution for a while, then taking them out and polishing them up.

The commonest solutions, both commercial and home-brewed, consist of ammonia and soap, the proportions varying somewhat according to personal liking. There is little advantage, except for convenience, in using a commercial concentrate. The mixture of ammonia and soap is still probably the most practical, although it has been found to bring out stresses in some early brass, causing occasionally severe distortion – for example, wheels dished from their centres or even separated at the rims. It is easy to be alarmist on this matter. The effect does not occur with brass after about 1800 and is rare even with older metal (though, unfortunately, it is unpredictable). The ammonia solution is cheap and very effective. If you do happen to be dealing with a really valuable old movement, then persevere with your brush (such as the suede brush) and metal polish alone; but generally your movement will come to no harm from, and cleaning will be assisted by, the traditional soaking. In our opinion it is a risk worth taking.

Grated toilet soap or even kitchen soaps with detergents are satisfactory. Household ammonia, bought from the chemist, must be diluted; one part of ammonia to eight parts of water is quite strong enough – a higher concentration will do little to improve cleaning and will increase the risk of damage. One part of turpentine substitute (white spirit) is a helpful but not essential addition. It is imperative that you cover all parts to be cleaned – including the backplate with projecting pillars. Depending on the shape of your tank, you will need at least a gallon of this solution. Parts which are not covered collect a high-water mark, a brown stain which is extremely difficult to remove.

It should be added that there are one or two commercial cleaners having an acid content (which should be stated on the label). While they can be used effectively, wiping on as directed, *never* try to use them, however much diluted, for soaking. Time-limits are easily overlooked and circumstances may intervene; we have witnessed the consequences of parts left too long in such a solution (dissolving away of every pivot, severe erosion of pinions and arbors) and can safely say that this is a mistake which one makes only once, so dire are the results.

The time required in the ammonia solution depends on the degree of tarnish, but six hours should be regarded as a maximum. It is helpful to string the parts, especially associated parts, together with wire before immersing them. The solution is most effective hot – but do not make the

Fig. 18   Wheels after soaking

mistake of boiling it, because this will deposit an unmanageable sludge on the parts and on your hands. It should also be covered or it will lose its effectiveness (it can in fact be re-used), and in any case the fumes are unpleasant.

The brass should emerge from its soaking yellow but dull. It must then be brushed immediately or the loosened dirt will readhere. (Fig. 18 shows some of the Burgess wheels at this stage). The rest is a matter of hard graft with metal polish and a fine rubber abrasive block. Wheel teeth will respond to the suede brush by hand. (Never be tempted to use any powered appliance since this will round the edges and distort the teeth. It is also dangerous.) Wheel spokes ('crossings') can be cleaned by pulling them over an end of 'chammy' leather held in the vice, or scraped with a broach. Be careful, if the rubber block is used, to brush parts clean afterwards; specks of rubber can become stuck in the pinions.

Longcase plates were not generally highly polished, but must be really clean, particularly in their holes. The pivot holes are cleaned with pointed pegwood (in an emergency, matchsticks are satisfactory), the point being twirled in a hole, scraped clean and then twirled again – and so on, until it leaves the hole quite free of discoloration.

In Victorian times it was discovered that a very attractive finish to plates could be had by 'graining' – rubbing them in dead straight lines with fine emery paper. You may find this on your movement, in which case it can be repeated, using fine paper on a cork block. However, this was seldom done before the nineteenth century and hardly ever on ordinary domestic longcase clocks. If you see it, you may suspect that it has been used to conceal defects (such as those seen in Fig. 14) rather than in the simple interests of a high-quality finish. If you meet graining, you cannot, of course, reverse it, but to introduce such a finish to your clock is almost certain to be 'wrong'.

Very few longcase clocks come with 'oil sinks' – cup-like countersinks round the holes. Some in the Scott clock have probably been added later. Their purpose is less to hold oil than to prevent its running over away from the pivots and down the plates. They can be cleaned with a specially made bit in the drill, with a round end of thick pegwood, or even with 'chammy' over the end of a cross-headed screwdriver.

Although it is not necessary it is usual to lacquer the main surfaces – the outsides at least of the plates, the pillars, the pallet cock and the pendulum bob (if it has a brass finish) to preserve the visual appearance. Lacquer can be applied to flat surfaces with cotton wool, but soft rag is better where the wool may catch. It dries superficially within seconds. Proceed in straight lines and only in extreme need return to places already tacky. The lacquer flows better if the parts are first warmed. Do not flood with lacquer – one loaded pad will do most of the clock, for lacquer goes a very long way. Should you have an accident and need to strip the coat, use methylated spirits.

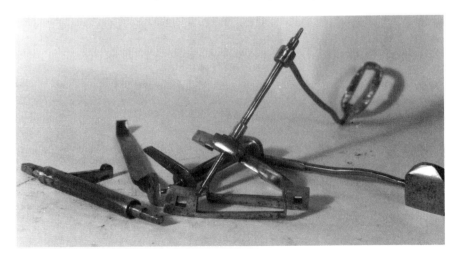

Fig. 19   Steelwork after cleaning

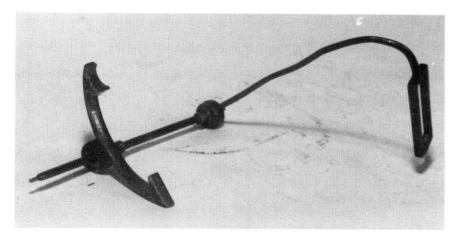

Fig.20   Scott pallets before cleaning

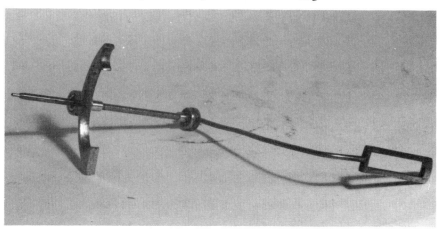

Fig. 21   Scott pallets after cleaning

Cleaning the Steel

The steel parts may be cleaned while the brass is soaking, although arbors from the train must, of course, be left till later.

Cleaning is a matter of diligent application with emery paper, emery buffs, the rubber block, and fine steel wool. There are no magic solutions, although 'biological' fluids are available which remove rust, leaving you still with a surface to finish. Probably the most difficult area is the pinions, especially where they are riveted to wheels. The traditional method is sharpened pegwood charged with emery or other abrasive powder. These powders are not now always available. A good substitute is fine car-valve grinding paste. Shape a slip of hardwood in the gap between pinion leaves, charge it, and rub. Brush off the sludge with methylated spirit. Scraping, with tips of files and broaches, also has a place. (The professional may use a powered hardwood lap, cut to the profile of the space between leaves and charged with abrasive.) Fig. 19 shows some cleaned steelwork from the Burgess clock and Figs. 20 and 21 show the Scott pallets before and after cleaning.

If you want a bright-looking thirty-hour chain, buy one from the suppliers. Close up any open links and measure the number of 'links per foot' – or, preferably, take greatwheel and pulley with you to the shop, for the measurement is not easy. Otherwise, soak the old chain in petrol for twenty-four hours and then rub it through an oily rag or steelwool, and close any open links. A chain generally opened will be found to have worn thin where the links rub and is best replaced, but if only a short length has stretched open there has probably been an accident with the weights and the links can be closed and re-used.

Screws can be cleaned with emery sticks in a powered chuck if available, or in a pin-chuck with a wire brush (Fig. 22). It is not usual to blue longcase screws, but mauled heads should be filed up and the slots may be improved with a file or hacksaw when a screwdriver is unlikely to hold reliably.

Fig. 22   Cleaning screws

5 Gear Train Repairs

Pivoting

To a large extent the timekeeping of the clock depends on reducing friction, for the effects of friction are irregular. The friction ought to be as nearly as is possible at the same level as in the original movement. This requires polished new pivots freely (but not sloppily) running in round, properly centred holes.

In this respect there is a certain contradiction between the present condition of a clock and its running record; a clock that has been constantly a good runner, a 'good' clock, may well present itself in a worse state of wear than one that has, for breakage or some other reason, run more intermittently over the years. We all know the heirloom proudly presented but in trouble – 'Can't imagine what's wrong with it, it's been going a treat for years'; that, in a word, is what is wrong with it – coupled, probably, with starvation of oil. The extensive – and extensively repaired – wear on the pivots and holes of the Scott clock spoke less of neglect than of a long satisfactory running life. In running, particles of metal rub off on and abrade the steel of pivots and pinions, the pivots become loose in their holes and the holes are worn off-centre. The gears are then misaligned and wear takes place there also. Restoring pivots and holes may be all that is necessary to bring an old clock back to life. So, tedious as the work may seem, producing no visible improvement as a reward, attention to pivots and holes is essential. The pivots of the eight-day Scott clock were in a particularly bad state, while with the Burgess thirty-hour movement it was the holes which desperately needed attention.

Longcase pivots are on the whole quite substantial compared with those of small clocks (let alone watches) and the work can be done with a fine file and pivot burnisher by hand. Grip a block of wood, preferably hardwood, in the vice and with a round file make a notch and channel in its top deep enough to house half of any particular wheel arbor's pivot. The set-up can be seen in Fig. 23. Where possible, hold the other end of the arbor in a pin-chuck – where this is not possible, do your best with fingertips. You then have to rotate, almost spin, the pivot to and fro in the channel, applying first the fine file or stone, and secondly the 'file' end of the burnisher, as the pivot is turning towards you.

Fig. 23   Polishing pivots by hand

The pivot is to be made smooth, polished and, above all, parallel – you will probably need the eyeglass to check its condition. A reinstated pivot of the Burgess scapewheel is shown in Fig. 24. Do not reduce the pivot needlessly – this will simply increase the work you have to do on the holes, and also weaken the pivot. On the other hand, do not shrink from removing metal if that is necessary to restore its true shape. The pivots are seen to first because you will be able to re-make the holes to receive the reduced, properly shaped pivots. Before you finally polish the pivot with the smooth end of the burnisher, rub the latter straight and hard across fine emery paper – it must have some edge to cut at all. All these operations can be carried out dry, but it is usual to lubricate the burnishing slightly, and for this there is no good substitute for a little spittle.

Sometimes – mainly through careless assembly – pivots are bent. It is difficult to straighten them, but worth the attempt. Use a hollow punch as lever, rather than pliers on the pivot. Test the corrected pivot by spinning its arbor between the plates. In this process, or for some other reason, a pivot may be broken. This poses a serious problem to the amateur – the technique is either to make a new arbor or to drill the existing one and insert a plug for the new pivot, and either approach needs a lathe. In these circumstances it may be best to pocket pride and take arbor and plates (the latter are essential) to a specialist. Makeshift solutions (such as a proud bush in the plate, or use of arbor caps which can be obtained with pivots in

Fig. 24   Polished pivot of Burgess scapewheel

various sizes) are unlikely to satisfy although, undeniably, they do work on occasion. Sadly it is the case that the finer the pivot, the more likely it is to break and the more tricky it may be to repair.

As has already been noted, some Scott pivots were in a lamentable state, being worn down so fine that they were quite disproportionate to their arbors and were unacceptably fragile. Two can be seen in Fig. 25. Such pivots require a lathe and probably specialist attention; effectively, they are broken pivots. In this case the arbors were drilled and new pivots inserted and fixed with Loctite. This necessitated, in due course, bringing their plate holes *up* to the required size. The new pivots can be seen in Fig. 26. While this was a repair not practicable in many homes, it must be stressed that pivot wear to this extent is not common. By far the more usual repair is to make the pivots finer by trueing them, and then to close the holes.

Bushing Holes

Only when you have completed work on the pivots can you fully assess what has to be done to the holes, although your preliminary examination will have identified some clearly worn or mutilated by previous attention. How do you distinguish holes needing repair? It is less a question of

Fig. 25   Eroded pivots on Scott clock

Fig. 26   Repaired pivots

measurement than of observation and 'feel'. It is not good workmanship, nor is it in the longterm interests of the clock, to bush holes unnecessarily; the notion that if every one is bushed, all the holes must be good and the clock will have been done a service should not be entertained. The eroded pivots of the Scott clock were a serious defect and must have occurred over a long period. During this period the holes had been bushed and re-bushed, disguising the real trouble and being done because it was quicker and easier than dealing with the pivots themselves. Judgement in this matter can be assisted by fact – some holes are more important, more subject to wear or more critical than others. The holes of the strike locking (the thirty-hour hoopwheel and eight-day locking or 'pallet' wheel) and those of hammer arbors are potential trouble-spots, as are those of the weight-bearing greatwheels. Where wheel and pinion are separated on an arbor, the hole at the pinion end often needs attention.

Fig.27   Arbors loose in enlarged plate holes

There is a further guide. A fair idea of the eccentricity of pivot holes can be gained from standing the arbor in its plate hole and observing the angle of deviation from the vertical. This, because of the lever effect of the arbor, will offer a large-scale gauge of the freedom in the hole. Try, of course, in several positions; what we are looking for in deciding whether a hole must be rebushed is eccentricity rather than looseness in itself – the eccentricity impairs the functioning of the gears. Since pivots and the lengths of arbors vary in size (and since the importance varies according to the position in the train) no particular movement at the top can be specified as excessive, but Fig. 27 shows two wheel arbors and Fig. 28 the countwheel detent arbor (from the Burgess clock) and the angles caused by their freedom. That of the greatwheel is excessive, while that of the

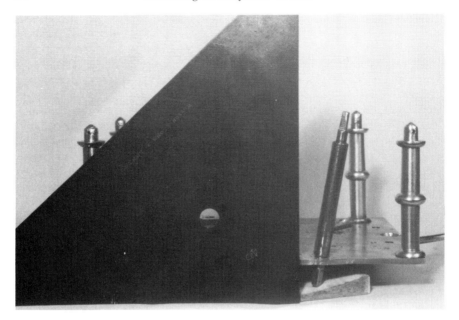

Fig. 28   Loose countwheel – detent arbor

warning wheel was felt to be acceptable. The detent, compared with the setsquare, is of course very bad. Naturally the pivot must be quite free in its hole, but not sloppy. A further check can be made by placing the suspect wheel and its neighbour between both plates and observing how they engage; if the driven pinion is held still and a gentle attempt is made to rotate the wheel, the pinion should not be able obviously to try riding up the teeth of the wheel, or the pivots to rise conspicuously in their holes. But always bear in mind the object of bushing. This is not to make a pivot tighter in its hole but to restore truth to the gearing. In fact, of course, a very loose hole means some departure from that truth. Incidentally, the fact that a hole is already bushed is no indication at all that it does not need bushing now – rather, it points to a recurrent trouble-spot.

Oval holes are corrected by enlarging 'backwards', balancing up the wear by making a larger hole round the original centre. This is known as 'drawing' the hole (Fig. 28). There is an appealing but expensive instrument – the 'depth tool' – available for locating exactly for any two arbors where the true centres should be for perfect meshing. But in a longcase clock the eccentricity can be sufficiently gauged by eye and allowed for. The hole is drawn backwards with a round file.

Meanwhile, a brass bush is selected which is a very close fit for, or just too small for, the pivot. It is then to the external size of this bush that the drawn hole is rounded and enlarged. For this the broach is used. It is vital that the hole be at right-angles to the plate; rotate your forearm, using the broach as axis and keeping constant watch on the angle of the broach; if the hole comes out not square to the plate, it will have to be enlarged for the pivot to run, and you will have undone much of your work. Broach the hole *from the inside of the plate* until the bush will fit to half the thickness of the plate (Fig. 29). The object is to rivet the bush into the plate and then to file the inside off level. Therefore the hole is countersunk lightly on the outside to make way for the riveted metal, after it has been hammered right into the hole on the inside. Because of the taper imposed by the broach, the bush will then be firmly riveted into the plate (Fig. 30). Sometimes the earlier punching-up marks are removed during bushing but, if not, they can be left as part of the clock's history.

Fig. 29   (*above*) Bushing a plate hole and Fig 29a (*below*) Drawing a worn hole

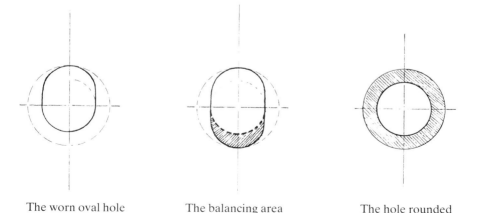

The worn oval hole   The balancing area   The hole rounded
                            filed out   and bushed

Fig. 30   Bushed plate hole

The bush was selected as a tight fit for the pivot and riveting will have tightened it further, so now with a small broach the pivot hole is gently eased to be a free fit for the pivot. Test this by trying the wheel and its neighbour between the assembled plates and adjusting the hole till the wheels run smoothly and quietly. The inner edge of the hole needs to be softened ('broken'). This can be effected by using a larger sized drill as a countersink, twisting it in the hand. Finally, the new hole is tidied up with a fine file and buff, bringing the edges of the bush dead level with the plate. A piece of photographic film with a hole in it is a well-tried way of protecting the plate itself from being scraped in this operation, and it can

Fig. 31   Straightened arbour in bushed hole

be followed by a strip of Sellotape. Ideally, the bush should be almost invisible and the wheel should run almost vertical. Fig. 31 shows the restored arbor angle of the greatwheel seen in Fig. 27.

You can see now why the pivots are trued up *before* the holes are corrected; altering the pivot for a new hole would result in just the loose fit which you are (partly) trying to correct. You can also see – if only from the amount of work involved – why, although all eccentric and very loose holes must be corrected, it is not desirable to carry out this radical work where it is inessential. Still, it is important. While not among the most immediately rewarding of jobs, pivoting and bushing are what the lawyers call a 'condition precedent'; if they are not properly seen to, all the other work will be time wasted and the clock will be at best unreliable.

Repairing Wheels

The Burgess clock had a damaged warning wheel (see Fig. 32). Wheels can often be repaired – they suffer less from general wear than from local flaws caused by accidents such as slipping ratchets. It is as well to check the wheels for missing teeth when they are cleaned, since this is quite a common fault and easily overlooked. Repair consists of soldering in new

Figs. 32–35 (*left to right*) Damaged warning wheel and repairing wheel teeth

teeth, although if more than three consecutive teeth are stripped it may be better to consider a new wheel, since it is difficult to file a number of teeth to size. In this case two teeth were missing. The first job is to make a slot for each tooth by filing the stubs flat and filing or sawing into the rim. An insertion on the large side is then made, soldered into place, filed to size and tidied up, when it should be almost invisible as a repair (Figs. 33–5). (It was an earlier custom to use steel pins in drilled holes in greatwheels, rather than to make brass teeth, but these are unsightly and lead to wear. They can be removed and replaced with brass teeth.)

In repairing wheels, handling the parts with the solder is inclined to be fiddly. It is best to select a strip of brass several inches long (Fig. 33) and with its thickness nearly equal to the width of the existing tooth; the end can then be soldered into place while you support the strip, cutting it off when it has set. This is a strong and effective repair which makes saving the wheel well worth while.

Wear and replacement in wheels and pinions

Although inability to cut wheels may seem to separate you pretty definitively from the true clockmaker, the clock repairer does not in fact spend much time cutting wheels. Usually a new wheel is cut only when one is missing, damaged wheels being repaired rather than replaced. So there is little point in regretting that you cannot cut your own wheels. Nowadays there are many small firms which will cut a wheel to your requirement quite cheaply – and mount it on a pinioned arbor, which could be quite a problem at home. Such makers advertise in the horological magazines (see Further Reading). The only essential is that you calculate the number of teeth and diameter at point of engagement of the missing item. The length of arbor and size of pivots can all be ascertained if you supply the plates and, to be certain, the pinion to be engaged. Calculating the number of teeth is outlined in Chapter 6 for the going train and in Chapters 7 and 8 for striking trains.

Pinions wear much more rapidly than wheels in clocks, as we have noted. The scape and fly pinions wear particularly badly, often enough to prevent going or striking from functioning without a much increased weight – which in the long run will worsen the situation. Filing out the troughs may give temporary relief but is often very difficult. Another expedient is to move the engaging wheel along its arbor so that it meshes with a new part of the pinion. This can be done by heating the collet, as collets were often soft-soldered into place, but with eighteenth century clocks at least the fixing can be very stubborn and to persist may invite damage. An alternative is to move the whole arbor by running the pivots in bushes made deliberately proud of the plates (Fig. 36), one on the inside and one on the outside, but this is not an attractive solution and does not look good. We have already noticed a version of it with the Burgess strike greatwheel (see Fig. 12), where riveted slabs of brass replace the bushes which would be used with lighter wheels. In the long term the best and only answer is to have a new pinion fitted (it can be drilled and fitted to the same, reduced, arbor) or to have a new arbor and pinion made. Again, advertisers will oblige.

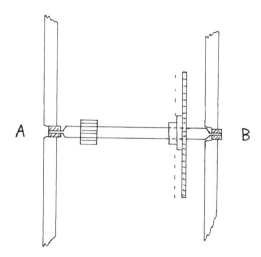

Fig. 36 Moving a wheel with proud bushes
A – Bush protruding inside of plate
B – Other bush recessed in plate

Worn scapewheel pinions are a common problem on longcase clocks. Typically the clock runs intermittently. When the train is examined at one of the steps it will be found that the scapewheel lacks power and will not spring back smartly if moved. In fact the wear takes such a form that the train jams at the escapement recoil (discussed in Chapter 6), when it briefly reverses direction. While the real solution is clearly a new pinion, this may sometimes be delayed by turning the wheel round very slightly against its own pinion, thus engaging different surfaces during escapement action.

A pinion which is actually broken (a leaf is broken off rather than there being general wear) is not so common on longcase clocks but it does occur, usually when the whole piece is weakened by wear and rust. It can be repaired by silver-soldering a new leaf in, but this is very intricate work and, again, replacement is the best answer.

Test Assembly

When you have overhauled the trains, lay the backplate, pillars up, across two battens or the backs of two books. With the wheels standing in their holes in this plate, lower the top plate into position and edge the pivots into their top holes. It is most easily done working from back (i.e. greatwheels) to front, finishing with fly and scapewheel. Take great care to ascertain which pivots are holding the floating top plate out of its proper location, so avoiding bent or broken pivots. An adapted pair of tweezers (see Fig. 37) is useful for pulling and pushing the pivots; bend the points inwards so that they overlap when closed. Another point to note in assembly is the ledge (shoulder on which the front bowspring will rest) on a centre arbor, which can long deceive one into believing that it is a pivot which is obstructing the fall of the plate into place. To avoid bent and broken pivots, take care with both ends of arbors; do not give so much attention to the pivot which you are inserting that you bend the one below which is already in its hole.

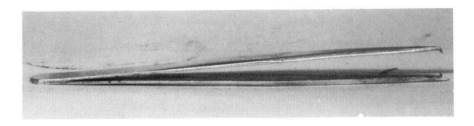

Fig. 37   Tool for inserting pivots into plate holes

New pins should be selected now for the pillars. Press them home and cut them to length, then remove them and file the cut off ends square before re-fitting. A pin should ideally protrude equally on each side of the pillar, but quite often there is very little room for dial feet and shorter pins have to be used in order to clear them (as will not be discovered until later). It is important that the pins, though in a temporary set-up, are pressed well home and the plate properly seated, because the freedom ('end-shake') of the pivots must be assessed in running conditions.

Test the freedom and smoothness of the trains by applying a finger to each greatwheel. The trains should gather speed and then coast quietly to a stop when power is removed. Again, if you hold the assembled plates horizontally and turn them right over, you should hear the pivots slide in their holes. Each arbor needs perceptible end-shake and also 'side-shake' (freedom to move sideways). This play is sensed rather than measured, but about 1 mm of endshake (in total) is usual. Testing each arbor for this individually, you may find that one is inclined to bind on a plate, and this must be rectified. If you have no lathe, this will have to be adjusted in the plates by lightly countersinking the hole of an offender. However, as a rule the cause will be that you have not adequately flattened the inside of a new bush, though sometimes one finds that an unaltered hole has always been on the high side, the arbor's shoulders being a shade long. Alternatively, there may be distortion in the plates, which can be rectified by strong-arm methods with the plate held between wooden blocks in the vice. Such distortion is usually apparent from the rocking of the top plate on the pillars or failure of the bottom plate's pillars to engage readily in the top plate's holes. This is also caused by bent or loose pillars; they can be straightened with a pipe as lever and may also need re-riveting with the hammer peen.

6 The Going Side

The Greatwheels and Ratchets

In a thirty-hour clock there is only one weight and one ratchet for winding. This ratchet (or 'clickwork') is invariably on the striking side, the chain being so looped that a single pulling action winds both trains (see Fig. 38). It is on the striking side for a very good reason – winding the going inevitably takes power off the train and leads to loss in timekeeping. The thirty-hour arrangement is a form of 'maintaining power' by which the going train is never deprived of power during winding; this is the one respect in which the clock is superior to all but exceptional eight-day longcase clocks.

The thirty-hour greatwheel driving pulleys are different for chain and rope driven clocks (see Fig. 39, and Part IV, Rope Drive), but all are subject to wear and to corrosion of the pins or spikes. The Burgess pulleys were not seriously worn and there was no need to renew them, but renewal is not an uncommon repair.

These pulleys were made of a brass core into which the spikes were driven and which was sandwiched between two brass discs, the whole being riveted together. To replace badly worn spikes the pulley must be dismantled. The rivets can sometimes be driven out, but more often they need to be centred with a punch and then drilled out. One can then see the worst as far as the spikes go. Usually it is a case of cutting off the remains and filing them smooth and fitting replacements. These can be made from wire nails filed or ground to blunt points for rope, or rounded for chain. The points for the rope are rounded so as not to tear the rope fibres. The pulleys can be re-assembled also with wire nails as rivets. Here it is often necessary to move the discs round as the original holes become too enlarged to grip a riveted end. Before hammering down the end (which may be about ½ mm proud before riveting) countersink any new holes to receive the riveted metal. (Thirty-hour ratchets are considered in Chapter 7 since they are generally part of the striking train.)

To obtain the longer going in an eight-day clock, *both* greatwheels are fitted with ratchets and the lines are coiled round barrels. The latter are usually grooved but those in the Scott clock were plain, and in this clock each barrel is, again less commonly, fitted with a guide for the line

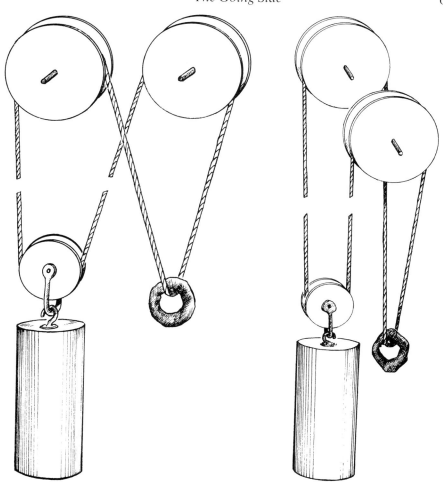

Plated movement side by side   Posted movement fore and aft

Fig. 38   Layout of thirty-hour rope or chain

(Fig. 40). It is not known whether any regional or dating significance attaches to these variations which are occasionally met. The barrel assembly consists of the barrel with its arbor driven in and ratchet teeth on one end, the greatwheel with pawl ('click') and spring attached, and a disc spring holding all together (Fig. 41). These have to be dismantled to be properly cleaned, but the arbor should be considered solid with the barrel. In the Scott clock one click-spring had broken and been replaced at some time with a piece of wire. This is a common fault and a workable but inelegant repair. It is better to make a new spring from scrap brass. Springs may be riveted or screwed and riveting had been used here, but it was

Fig. 39   Chain (*left*) and rope thirty-hour driving pulleys

decided that screwing would make a better job. (The same option exists with the spring disc. This may be pinned or screwed in place. If pinned, the pin may well have to be drilled out and then a new pin or screw fitted. Obstinate discs can be removed by levering up the edge of the disc and sawing through the pin between disc and wheel.) The design for the new spring was marked out on paper which was then stuck to a piece of brass (Fig. 42) and cut out with the piercing saw. The finished spring was beaten with a hammer to harden it, which in itself produced the required curve (Fig. 43). The clicks themselves (visible in Fig. 41) vary in shape, and the better ones have long tails to facilitate letting down the weights if required. They are, of course, a free fit in the greatwheels, the back end of the crucial screw or rivet being hammered over. Replacement clicks can be bought but more often they have to be made to style. Attention must be given to fit and rivet; a sloppy fit will wear the ratchet or lead to slipping, while a screw or rivet coming out under power spells disaster.

   The lines are most easily fitted at this stage but, once fitted, have to be kept out of harm's way lest entanglement causes an accident. Gut lines are easier to handle than wire or synthetic lines but all are adequate in strength. Wire lines are strongest but tend to mark the barrel. Gut lines should be well oiled before use. To instal, first make sure that the barrel holes are smooth, filing them out if not (this is where most wear takes

Fig. 40   Eight-day line fitting with guide

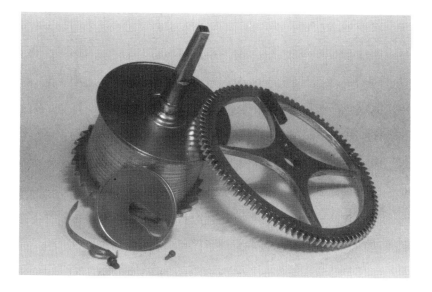

Fig. 41   Eight-day barrel assembly

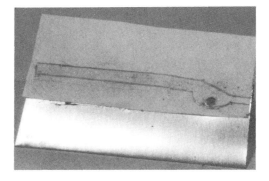

Fig. 42   Replacing a click spring

Fig. 43   The click spring completed

place). Thread an end from outside into the barrel, and with a wire hook through the big hole in the end of the barrel catch the line and pull it out, making a simple knot in it and then returning it. With wire it may be felt necessary, though is not really desirable, to soften the wire with heat before knotting. With gut and synthetic lines the ends can be 'mushroomed' on a hot knife so that the knots cannot come unfastened.

The Pendulum

Usually the pendulum bob is cleaned with other brass-work but sometimes, especially on Victorian clocks, it is painted, as are many pendulum rods, which may be strips rather than rods. Rods may be cleaned up with emery paper and restored as desired with matt black paint. It is difficult, and hardly necessary, to straighten every bend in wire pendulum rods, but they should be straight overall.

A smooth regulating action is essential – the bob must slide down the rod by its own weight and the bob hole must be opened with broaches and files till this is achieved. Rods end in a short length of often tapered flat steel and this shank is screwed onto them, usually with a 5BA thread. Where an old rod's thread is hopelessly worn and the nut slipping, it may be preferable to replace this flat rather than to make a new and finer thread on the old shank. There can be difficulty in fitting bobs to shanks. Patient filing is the answer, and both shank and bob hole may have to be filed where either bob or shank is being replaced.

The regulating nut, which is most often a square of thick brass, must hold on the thread. You may find heavy punch marks on the nut, made in an effort to tighten it. Such nuts are best replaced with a similarly tapped brass square. Sometimes the lower hole in the bob is distorted, the brass cover being forced away from the lead. This has to be corrected as well as possible with a mallet, but a larger nut may be necessary.

The most fragile part of the pendulum is its suspension spring. This spring must be undistorted and straight and, if there is any doubt, an old one should be replaced as it can stop the clock. Sometimes the new spring will be too long for the crutch to locate properly and a new spring will have to be adapted. New springs are available with or without the lower brass end which engages with the crutch. Normally the original lower end can be retained when replacing a spring. The riveting pins are punched out, and then a hole must be made in the new spring for the new rivet. It is undesirable to soften the spring by heating it and not easy to drill it without. The best plan is to use a cube of scrap metal, drilling it to the appropriate size right through and then sawing across the hole (Fig. 44); this forms a jig into which the end of the spring can be eased, the hole being punched through from above with a square-ended punch, which can be made from scrap rod or a wire nail of suitable thickness.

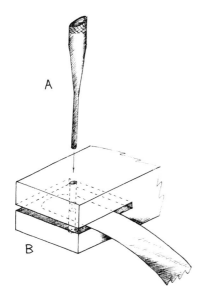

A

B

Fig. 44   Punching a hole in spring steel
A – Flat-faced punch
B – Split block with hole for punch
The split block may, if the holes are
unworn, be the suspension block itself.

If the pendulum is missing, establishing its length is discussed in Part IV; the length is critical to the timekeeping of the clock. As for weight, a thirty-hour bob may be smaller than an eight-day bob and weigh about 2½ lb compared with 3½–4 lb, being about 3½'' compared with 5'' in diameter. The size of bob is not critical either to going or to timekeeping, though the heavier bob is to be preferred. All pendulum components are available, as is a complete new pendulum, from suppliers. Good quality can be had and it is hardly necessary to go to the lengths of making a new pendulum.

Gearing

Where one wheel drives another, the relationship of their speeds will be that of their sizes; if the driving wheel is half the diameter of the other, it will revolve twice as fast. Provided the teeth are all of the same size ('module'), the same ratio will be contained in the numbers of wheel teeth; a pinion of 10 driving a wheel of 20 will revolve twice as fast (though such low ratios are not normally found in clockwork).

The going train of a clock follows this principle. The scapewheel revolves once a minute and carries the seconds hand – if there is one. (If there is not, the wheel may not be designed to turn in exactly a minute.) The wheel carrying the minute hand (which in the Burgess clock is a centre wheel, but is not always so in thirty-hour clocks – see Part IV) must revolve once in 60 minutes, so the ratio required so far is 1:60. We can set out the going trains for our examples as follows (wheels above, pinions below):

	Great	Centre	3rd	Scape
Burgess	72	60	56	30
		(10)	8	7
Scott	96	60	56	30
		(8)	8	7

These are frequently used trains. Note that the greater duration of the Scott eight-day clock is due to winding the line onto the barrel, instead of just passing once round the pulley – the trains are essentially the same. To calculate the overall ratio, the wheel teeth are multiplied together, then the pinion leaves, then the product of the teeth divided by the pinion leaf total; however, the wheel teeth are also multiplied by two, because only half a tooth's space on the scapewheel is released at each beat of the pendulum – there are sixty 'ticks' for thirty teeth. The overall ratio (to the centre wheel) is 3,600, the number of seconds in an hour, because these pendulums swing in one second (see Part IV).

Of course the 60:1 reduction from seconds hand to minute hand could theoretically have been carried out by one 600 toothed wheel driving a 10-leaved pinion, but the wheel would have been too big and would have revolved in the wrong direction; these constraints are always present for clockmakers.

The minute hand's one revolution per hour must then be reduced to one revolution in twelve hours (for the hour hand), and this is done by wheels mounted separately on the front plate and known as 'motion wheels'. As the hands are required to be concentric, two wheels are needed so that both hands move clockwise, although again a single wheel could otherwise have made the desired reduction. The striking is let off by a pin in the surface-mounted ('minute') wheel, or by a twelve-toothed starwheel attached to the last wheel when the clock has only an hour hand. (The motion-work of single-handed and three-wheel thirty-hour clocks is different. See Part IV.)

The final ratio is concerned with making the power or winding last a tolerable time with some spare (thirty hours representing a day and eight days representing a week). This is effected by having a large greatwheel drive a small pinion.

Other, but in principle similar, arrangements are made where there are only three wheels in the train, no centre wheel, and the minute hand driven at the front by the greatwheel arbor. In these cases, of course, the greatwheel is not concerned *solely* with power-supply and duration, but is a calculated part of the time train through from the scapewheel to the hand – i.e. it has to be included when calculating the overall ratio, for example to establish the length of pendulum needed.

Naturally, although variations are found, there were a number of recognized standard trains used again and again. However, it should be noted that the pendulums of thirty-hour clocks do not, especially where there is no seconds hand, all swing in exact seconds, and the scapewheels do not always have thirty teeth (both being normal on eight-day clocks). The presence of one of these departures is indicated when the ratio to the minute hand arbor wheel, calculated as above, is not 3600:1.

All this need not concern you very much if your clock has no wheels missing and if you are reasonably sure that it has the original pendulum or one that is appropriate. You can, of course, experiment with trial rods of different lengths and do no harm. Otherwise, however, you may need to do some calculation. It is a case of working from the known (what you already have, and the fixed requirements for timekeeping) to the missing factor – although you will find the commoner trains set out all ready for you in several books listed under Further Reading. An aid or a check on deductions made exists in the space available for a missing wheel since, as has been said, the space is directly related to the number of teeth provided that all the teeth are of the same size (which, until quite modern clocks, they generally were). The total space between the plate holes will be the radius of the existing pinion + the radius of the missing wheel. The ratio of the diameter of the pinion to the deduced diameter of the missing wheel will be the same as the ratio of their numbers of teeth – and the number of the pinion's teeth is known. Such measurements of course conceive of wheels and pinions as rollers; in practice, they intersect and an allowance for this has to be added when making them. Specifically, this depends on the cutter to be used, but generally you need to add 3.1 to the 'pitch diameter' of a wheel and 1.7 to that of a pinion to arrive at their gross size including overlap.

Motion Wheels

With two hands there are three motion wheels (disregarding any for date and moon) –a 'cannon pinion' with a pipe riding on the central arbor, a 'minute wheel' (sometimes given other names) gearing with it and (usually) offset to the right, and a big 'hour wheel' riding on the cannon's pipe or a supporting bridge (see Fig. 47). Each wheel has ancillary functions. The cannon pinion is usually part of the clutch mechanism – it is loose on the central arbor but is pressed against a bowed spring ('bowspring'); through this pressure the clock drives the hands, but they can also be turned independently to set to time. The minute wheel in eight-day clocks (and in thirty-hour clocks with two hands) lets off the striking by means of a pin in its rim. The hour wheel may have a similar pin – or a shaped nib – which operates the date indicator and moon phases. On an eight-day clock the hour wheel is usually composite (Fig. 48) with the snail attached either rigidly or by the friction of a disc spring, as here in the Scott clock. This enables the hour hand also to be set, though in practice this should not be necessary.

This is the arrangement in a clock such as the Scott, where there is a centre wheel. Where there is not, or where there is only one hand, there are different arrangements of motion work driven from the going greatwheel (see Part IV).

Motion-work seldom needs repair, apart from replacing missing drive pins, but it quite often stops a clock, although there was no problem in the Burgess and Scott clocks. The source of the trouble is usually the incorrect fitting of the bowspring (which should be bent convex to the plate); bad fitting of the minute hand (see Chapter 10 – Fitting Hands); or a minute wheel stud which is loose in the plate. Sometimes also the hour wheel pipe has to be eased onto the cannon pinion with a broach. The load of date and moonwork, which are driven from the motion work, may also prove too much for the weight if not properly overhauled. Motion-work is free to the touch, so far as wheel teeth allow, when the clock is running; if it feels stiff or jammed solid (unless date or moon are just changing) there is something wrong.

The Escapement

As has already been said, to those unfamiliar with clocks it seems that in some way the pendulum itself *drives* the going. Nothing could be further from the truth; the pendulum actually *stops* the clock at every second and is in fact *driven by* it; without the weighted gear train, the pendulum would swing on its own for a few minutes at best. It is the escapement which keeps it going.

The escapement consists of the pallets, attached to the crutch, and the escapement wheel ('scapewheel'). Its action can be most easily followed by setting up the scapewheel between plates and fitting the pallets to their cock by hand. You will see that each scapewheel tooth has two faces, one radial and one sloped and usually curved. In this 'recoil' escapement (which is all but universal in longcase domestic clocks: see Part IV), the sloped face leads and meets the pallets, which are so shaped that teeth are alternately intercepted and released with each swing of the pendulum. The action can be followed in Figs. 45 a–g, which show the escapement of the Scott clock in action behind a substitute perspex plate.

Here a special plea is made – indeed, a warning given. You are probably reading this book because yours is a practical nature – you can mend the mixer, put in a wall-plug, etc. You may well believe that you have a 'feel' for handiwork. You may also believe that an ounce of this 'feel' is worth at least a pound of the theoretical stuff in books – perhaps you do not always read the instructions. You may even identify with craftsmen of the past – surely these clocks were not built step by step with a handbook at their side?

Any of these assumptions may be justified, but shed them in dealing with escapements. You *must* know what 'drop' and 'depth' are, and you must know the difference between 'entry' and 'exit' pallets. There must be good reasons for any alterations which you make and they must be accompanied by measurement. To sail in with the feeling that 'it's a bit loose here' or 'binding' there is to court disaster, either in the form of a movement barely alive, or with pallets so mutilated that they have to be replaced. Your 'feel' may well be an invaluable bonus, but do not start with it alone.

Consider Fig. 45. The pallet which catches a tooth on its outside, underneath, is known as the 'entry pallet', and the pallet which catches a tooth inside, on the way out, is known as the 'exit pallet'. The pallets are shaped so that each wheel tooth, as it passes through, is first stopped by them and then gives them a little push or 'impulse'. These tiny regular impulses are what keep the pendulum going. Meanwhile – between the stopping and the impulse – each tooth is pushed backwards slightly by the ongoing pendulum via the crutch – this is the 'recoil' from which the escapement takes its name.

For the clock to keep going, the escapement must carry out this dual function of interrupting ('locking') and impulsing and, for it to do so, the condition of the scapewheel and pallets is very critical. The first focus of your attention should be the wheel. Time and again one comes across pallets which have been put through exquisite tortures when the real fault is in the wheel. Many quite modern clocks stop from wear or untruth in their scapewheels and this is even more likely in a clock at least 150 years old.

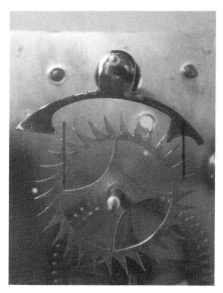

a	b	e	f
c	d	g	

Fig. 45a-g   The working of a recoil escapement (vertical lines are a guide to movement):

(a)   entry pallet engaged, with recoil, pendulum completes swinging to right; (b)   entry pallet released, pendulum swinging to left, note 'drop' at exit pallet; (c)   exit pallet engaged, pendulum swinging to left; (d)   recoil as pendulum swings further to left; (e)   exit pallet released as pendulum swings to right, note 'drop' (exaggerated) on entry pallet; (f)   entry pallet engaged, pendulum swings to right; (g)   recoil at entry pallet as pendulum completes rightward swing.

The Scapewheel

It cannot be over-emphasized that the wheel must deliver its tiny impulse through every tooth. Put the arbor between the open jaws of a vice with one pivot resting on each jaw and turn the wheel. A tendency to return rapidly to the same point of balance indicates that the arbor is bent, and it will be better to remedy this, gently bending until the wheel is in poise, than to shorten teeth on the 'heavy' side. It is also possible to check for a bend by mounting the arbor in the chuck of a good hand-drill held in the vice – the free pivot should not describe a circle – but cheap drills are too loose and untrue for this to be reliable. Again, you can grip the end of the arbor in a pin-chuck and turn it against a really flat surface such as glass.

You can see that, if some of the scapewheel teeth are short, in extreme cases they may fail to lock or, more probably, impulse will not be delivered; the pallets obviously have to be distanced so that they will clear all the teeth, and this in practice means that they will be set for the long ones while action on the others will be unsatisfactory. A slightly irregular scapewheel can be an elusive troublemaker later on when the overhauled clock is found to run only for a short time, and it is best to cover this possibility from the outset.

Ideally, the wheel is set up in the lathe and lightly turned or filed until all its teeth are exactly the same length. Then the shape of blunted teeth is corrected by hand with a file – touching only the curved tooth backs, for the exactly-measured radial faces must never be altered. Without a lathe one method is, with the train powered and in place, to hold a fine file against the revolving scapewheel. Another method is to use a piece of paper or card. Push the un-pinioned end of the scapewheel arbor through so that the wheel lies flat on the surface and carefully, with a needle or very sharp pencil, mark the positions of all the tooth tips. Also, using a pen, mark one tooth and its place on the card so that the wheel can be replaced in the same position. Then stick your card to a piece of thin wood or cork and centre the point of a pair of compasses in the hole made by the arbor and filled in by the backing wood. Find by experiment the radius for the shortest tooth and draw an exact circle, then mark the teeth that need to be shortened to bring them down to the line. Making these alterations with a file, you will obtain the first necessity of the escapement, a trued scapewheel.

The Pallets

Pallets are removable without dismantling the clock and thus are vulnerable. If your clock has no pallets it would usually be advisable to have a new set made. This work is outside the scope of this book, although pallet blanks are available from suppliers. Several books listed under

Further Reading give instructions for making pallets to size, however, and some amateurs with a fair range of tools and a good deal of time could produce their own set.

However pitted and worn your pallets may be, you can assume that their basic angles and lengths are correct and intact, at least where unworn at a side, and these have to be restored all over. Fig. 46 shows a suspect set of pallets – from the Burgess clock; though broader and heavier than those from an eight-day clock (in line with similar differences between the scapewheels), pallets with so little wear cannot, in view of the rough state of other parts of the movement, be original. However, they are in keeping and proved quite satisfactory.

Fig. 46   pallets from the Burgess clock

Badly pitted pallets can be re-faced with pieces of mainspring, but even if you have no such steel available (assortments of alarm clock springs can sometimes be had from suppliers) the pallets should be levelled to the lowest point, carefully retaining the original angles. Pallets of good quality have been hardened and you will find that a file makes little impression. If it can be avoided it is not desirable to soften them, so one should resort to stoning (rubbing with a tool-sharpening slip-stone is satisfactory) before polishing with file and burnisher.

Re-facing pallets is one of the few jobs in clockwork where soft solder is used. It may be done in cases of severe wear or where, on balance, the possibly original set should be kept. Otherwise replacement is preferable.

Selecting a mainspring slightly wider than the pallet and of appropriate thickness, it is easiest to hold a long strip of the spring, solder the end in place, and then to break off the unwanted length. Do not heat the pallet any longer than is necessary, and try to ensure that the solder forms only a thin coating. For this sort of job Baker's Fluid flux is helpful; paint it on to spring and pallet and apply a little solder, ensuring that it flows (some modern springs are not suitable for soldering). After 'tinning' the surfaces in this way, and if necessary filing down surplus solder, bring them together and apply heat to the join. Once the face is fixed in place, file the edges close to the shape of the pallet. The repair should be almost invisible.

Even if they do not require re-facing, pallets need to be polished until wear or scratch-marks from emery disappear. This is carried out with the burnisher, holding the pallets in a vice and using considerable pressure and some spittle. Be very careful after working on pallet faces that you leave no burrs at the edges; these can be felt, but reliance is better placed on an eyeglass.

Sometimes it is possible to avoid re-facing by moving either scapewheel or pallets on their arbors, to which they are soldered. But for this there must be a good unworn area of pallet available and it must be possible (often it is not) to move the parts concerned.

Adjusting Drop

'Drop' is the distance travelled by the next tooth to fall on a pallet as the opposite tooth is released. It is measured just as one tooth is released (see Fig. 45b). In that time the wheel is free of the pallets and delivers no impulse; drop is wasted time and energy from the point of view of keeping the pendulum swinging. Some such freedom is inevitable or the wheel could not move, but it has to be reduced to a minimum. (This is why it is sometimes supposed that a clock returned from repair is no better, sounds weak and will not go for long; it is quieter because the drops have been reduced and it will in fact run better.)

Obviously drop occurs on both the entry and exit pallets, and in fact the drop on each should be the same. Clearly it will vary if the scapewheel is not perfectly regular, so for the wheel to pass through the pallets they have to be set to allow the passage of the teeth giving the greatest acceptable drop. It is impossible to prescribe a minimum drop since each example varies, but certainly no more than half a milimetre should be needed, and with a good scapewheel it can and should be less. Measurement can be by feeler gauge or a thin piece of scrap metal – or you can reduce the drop until the wheel stops for lack of clearance and then back off. (As already mentioned, lack of clearance can also be produced by an individual thick, blunt wheel tooth, whose back should be filed.)

The drop on the entry pallet is set by the height of the pallets, adjustable at the pallet cock within existing screwholes if possible, or filing them upwards as little as possible. Sometimes it has been crudely adjusted in the past by bending the pallet arbor down, in which case you should straighten it and will probably need to re-face the pallet. The drop on the exit pallet is reduced by closing the pallets or re-facing. As already noted, many of these pallet sets are hardened – shown by a file's barely marking them – and before closing must be softened by heating to red heat, avoiding the actual pallets as far as possible. To close, balance the pallets across an open vice, protecting the under-surface from the jaws, and strike them in the middle with a strip of wood (such as a buff handle) under a hammer. Do be careful, however, to measure the exact gap between the pallets before doing this, and proceed cautiously – the gap is much harder to enlarge.

It is clear on consideration that altering one pallet will also affect the other, and therefore it is best not to make the full estimated change in one go. Bear in mind also that the pallets must embrace exactly $X + \frac{1}{2}$ teeth (X being as observed – usually 7 or 8). While closing the pallets will alter their angles, the change should be too small to justify tampering with the angles themselves.

This section concludes, as it began, with a gentle warning: the distances involved in adjusting even a badly worn escapement are very small, and work done can often not be reversed. Proceed gradually, step-by-step, making a note of what you are doing.

7   Countwheel Striking

Working of the Burgess Clock's Striking

The Burgess clock, like virtually all thirty-hour clocks, uses the oldest striking system, that of the 'countwheel' (or 'locking plate' – something of a misnomer, since it is in fact essential that the countwheel does *not* lock the train but only indicates where it is to be locked). There are various patterns and uses of this mechanism (see Part IV), but the principle is always the same. So is the distinctive 'user' feature of the system, that each hour can be struck only once, after which it will be followed by the next hour; there is no way in which the same hour can be struck twice. If the striking should be out of phase with the time shown by the hour hand, it is best to release the train and 'strike it round' to the appropriate point. (Hour hands on many clocks cannot be moved without damage. There are exceptions, but it is best to play safe and not turn them.)

The main striking parts of the Burgess striking mechanism are shown in Figs. 47–50, where they are ready for assembly. While by no means rare, the release and warning and arrangements are not those most commonly found (outlined in Part IV). The sequence of striking an hour can be followed through in Figs 51 a–d. First, the lifting and warning piece (the latter protruding into the train) is being raised by the pin on the minute wheel, on which rests a link piece which is on the same arbor as the locking piece, at the back, in the gap of the hoopwheel. The lifting continues until the warning piece is in position to intercept the pin on the warning wheel. Through the link piece the locking at the hoopwheel is released and the train runs briefly until the warning pin strikes the warning piece (Fig. 51b). (At this point the countwheel detent, not shown here, is rising out of its slot in the countwheel behind the back plate.) Precisely on the hour the minute wheel has progressed so that the lifting piece falls off its pin (Fig. 51c) and the train is free to run and strike – you will see that the locking piece now rides on the hoopwheel's rim. When the countwheel detent is over the next slot in the countwheel, the locking piece can drop back into the hoopwheel gap (Fig. 51d) and the train comes to rest for another hour.

The key point is that, for the train to lock and striking to cease, a notch on the countwheel must coincide with the gap in the hoopwheel. The graduated high sections of the countwheel correspond to numbers of revolutions of the hoop or locking wheel, and this latter wheel makes one

Fig. 47

Fig. 48

Fig. 49

Fig. 50

Figs. 47–50   Main parts of Burgess striking (omitting countwheel)

THE SEQUENCE OF COUNTWHEEL STRIKING

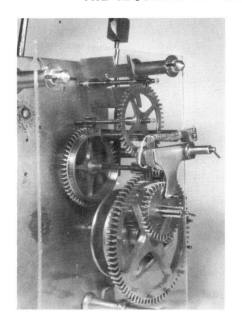

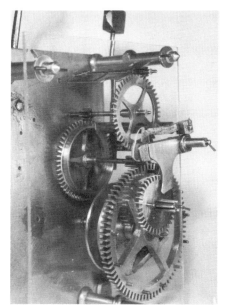

revolution for each blow of the hammer caused by the pins on the revolving greatwheel. All this is effected by the gearing of the striking train, which we will consider shortly.

Warning

Warning is a subsidiary release of the train prior to striking, the train being held by the meeting of the intercepting warning piece and the pin on the warning wheel (next to the fly). It is needed for two reasons. First, without warning there would be no assurance that the device which releases the train (the lifting piece) would be out of the way when striking was due to cease – the striking could run on over the right number of blows. Study of the lifting action will show why this is so – the lifting piece could still be held raised by its lifting pin after striking has begun and after it should have finished. Secondly, warning is a safeguard with the countwheel system; a properly adjusted warning release means that when the full release eventually occurs, the detent cannot fall back into the same countwheel slot (since the train has moved a little to reach warning). This may sound a little complicated at the moment, but you may need to re-think the working if, as may well happen, your striking is not reliable when first assembled.

Gearing

There is nothing haphazard about the gearing of the striking train; most of it is determined by requirements as fixed as those of the timekeeping train, and the dimensions of missing wheels can be calculated in a similar way. The over-riding requirement we have already seen – the ratio of the hoopwheel to the countwheel. The latter has to make one revolution in 12 hours, during which 78 (12+11+10 etc.) blows are to be struck, and the hoopwheel must revolve 78 times, one for each blow of the hammer; so the ratio of these two wheels is to be 78:1. This is accomplished in two stages – the ratio of the wheel attached to the back of the countwheel itself to the pinion on the extended arbor of the greatwheel, and the ratio of the greatwheel's teeth to the leaves on the hoopwheel pinion. For the Burgess movement these can be set out as follows:

Fig. 51a Lifting pin raising lifting piece, train not yet unlocked for warning; (b) warning set, link-lever to locking engaged, detent on hoopwheel rim, train held at warning with (not shown here) the detent raised from the countwheel slot; (c) the lifting piece has fallen, releasing the warning pin, and the train runs; (d) the train is locked, the locking piece lodged in the hoop and (behind the backplate) the detent having fallen into a countwheel slot

Countwheel	Greatwheel	Hoopwheel
48	78	56
	8	6

This is in fact a very common striking train. The size of the countwheel and its wheel, and that of the pinion on the greatwheel arbor, do not permit great variation, though pinions of 10 and 12 (with corresponding countwheel wheels of 60 and 72) are common, and one example of a 14 pinion with an enormous (4 inch) countwheel of 96 has been seen. There are always (as here) 13 hammer-lifting pins on the greatwheel – a factor of 78.

Towards the faster end of the train the gearing also has to meet a set requirement – the wheels must always be in the same position when locked; otherwise the train could not be relied upon to lock precisely when the detent was positioned in a countwheel slot. This is also necessary for correct 'warning' before full release and striking. This gearing therefore must have integral ratios. Apart from this, the gearing to the warning wheel and fly is a matter of taste, since it governs the speed of striking. The Burgess ratios are as follows:

Hoopwheel	Warning	Fly
56	48	
	7	6

Over the years that the longcase clock was produced, preference tended towards slower striking and higher ratios. Also, flies developed from a heavy fly-wheel type (usual in posted movements) to a broader, lighter form of air-brake (which was often cut away to clear the pallets).

Bearing in mind that the sizes of the wheels as indicated by the plate holes will confirm calculations, it is not too difficult to establish the counts of missing striking wheels. This is required most often for the countwheel-wheel and loose greatwheel pinion; the countwheel and its wheel are riveted together but held to the stud on the backplate only by a pin and some form of spring clip, while the pinion is nearly always held in place only by the countwheel overlapping it. Thus one or both parts may be missing. Often the size of the wheel will be clear from marks on the backplate. The ratio is 6:1. Occasionally the pinion is cut out of the greatwheel arbor as four pins. Otherwise the pinion is likely to have been of six or eight leaves. You need to tell suppliers the number of teeth and the diameter at the point of meshing (on the 'pitch circle'); they have a formula for deriving the size of wheel teeth from this data, but a carbon rubbing or photo-copy of the plate will also help. The countwheel itself is discussed below.

Repairs

Because the striking parts of the Burgess clock are relatively modern compared with those of many longcase clocks, they were not very seriously worn. But the abruptness of surfaces meeting which is inherent in striking – the locking of the train at warning and full locking, the violent action of heavy hammers and stiff springs in these clocks – does often produce wear which is sufficient to prevent their operating properly. Having already noted the tendency to distortion of hoopwheel and hammer pivot holes, we will now look at other danger-points – to which, of course, must be added the tendency of these mainly steel parts to be eaten away by rust.

THIRTY-HOUR GREATWHEEL AND RATCHET

Repair of the greatwheels generally was discussed in Chapter 6. The striking wheel bears the hammer pins and winding ratchet.

With a very old clock – particularly with posted clocks, which have large bells, heavy hammers and very strong hammer springs – the pins on the greatwheel become worn, half the pin often being worn flat. This was not the case on the Burgess clock, but it is easily remedied when it occurs and it is best then to replace the full set of pins, punching (or if necessary drilling) out the old ones. Replacements can be made from wire nails or, better, silver steel rod or 'pivot steel' (available in assorted sizes from suppliers). It is not a good idea to use taper pins. The back ends can be riveted over (though pivot steel is too hard for this) and, if care is taken in broaching to a tight fit, the pins will be strong enough if driven in with a drop of Loctite 601. They must be cut to length and the ends stoned square – pivot steel is best cut by nicking with a file and then breaking. The arbor can be held in a revolving drill chuck to facilitate sizing and finishing; pins sharp from cutting, or of different lengths, are an unattractive sight.

Fig. 52   Burgess strike
greatwheel and ratchet

Fig. 53   Types of thirty-hour ratchet

The greatwheel ratchet must be checked and made good if necessary. The Burgess clock (Fig. 52) did not feature the commonest type of ratchet (the forms are discussed in Part IV and illustrated in Fig. 53). The most usual ratchet is that on the left, to which the greatwheel itself is pressed – the raised nib on the spring catches on the spokes of the wheel in one direction and brushes past in the reverse. The action is noisy and almost seems designed to wear out quickly. Moreover, the springs are very difficult to repair (see Part IV). The alternative, as in the Burgess, is an arrangement with ratchet wheel and pawl.

THE LOCKING-PIECE

The locking-piece (or 'hoopwheel detent') is repeatedly subject to hard blows and its condition often reflects the fact. (It can be seen, attached to its arbor, in Fig. 50 and, in action, in Figs. 51 a–d). There are very precise conditions to be met here and a little wear can upset things badly. The locking-piece tip is either down in the gap of the hoop, locking the train, or up and riding on the outside of the hoop. It has also, in the most common design, itself to effect the change from one position to the other. This it does by its sloped face as the edge of the hoop slides against it before the train is temporarily arrested by the warning-piece. Through wear, this critical sloped face is inclined to be extended, in which case locking will be unreliable – the clock will tend irregularly to strike two hours together ('mis-locking'). Unless the vertical face *is* vertical, the hoop will be inclined to slide off it. The piece is also apt to be worn away at the tip. In this case the locking-piece is not raised high enough onto the hoop rim, so that the countwheel detent sticks on the countwheel, either jamming the train or giving a false count of 'one'. Thus it can be seen that the difference between the high and low positions of the locking piece should be at least equal to the difference between the countwheel detent's height inside and outside the countwheel's slots. This may appear obvious, but the locking piece is difficult to watch in operation and the point is often overlooked when there is a case of mis-locking and mis-counting, when the trouble is wrongly sought in countwheel or countwheel detent. Usually the piece can be re-shaped by filing, but compensatory bending to lower it may be needed.

THE HOOPWHEEL

The hoop, the projecting rim on the hoopwheel, may be accepted with wear at its leading edge, but not with pieces broken off. A common 'repair' to this edge is the insertion of a vertical pin, which has the advantage of avoiding replacement of the authentic hoop. The hoop is riveted in by means of its integral feet. Incomplete and loose hoops are quite common and will cause mis-locking. As the strength depends on there being rivets all round, it is generally better to replace an actually damaged rim – which is not difficult with a strip of thick brass – than to try to repair it. You may find the riveting difficult and here *small* amounts of solder may perhaps be tolerated, but to solder the whole rim in place is an act of vandalism. Except that obviously it must easily receive the locking-piece, the size of the gap in the rim is not critical.

THE FLY

New flies can be filed from solid – appropriate mainly to the thick ones – made up from two brass blades linked by suitable bushes, or bought in blank form. They are a loose fit on their arbors but held friction-tight by a springy strip of brass usually riveted to one side and running in a groove on the arbor where the latter is crossed. (Fig. 54 shows the Burgess fly.) These springs often need tightening or replacement, and this is done by riveting on a slip of brass hammered hard. They cannot be tightened in situ.

Fig. 54   Burgess fly

The idea is plain – as the train revolves, the friction grip causes the fly to revolve too and brake the motion but, when the fly is suddenly arrested, the fly should run on under its own momentum, absorbing the shock to the gears and reducing wear. Hence the 'clickety-clack' sound after a church clock strikes – it is the fly, here fitted with a sprung ratchet, running on. However, it is clear from observation and from the heavy wear which affects fly pinions that often the device is only partially, if at all, effective. Heavy flies tend to work best in this respect, but their disadvantage is that their potential for wear is greater. If, on the other hand, the spring is too loose, the blows of striking will be irregularly spaced.

Finally, it is always wise to pay attention to the poise of a fly; balance it across the jaws of a vice and, provided that the arbor is not bent (as it may well be in the fragile area of the groove), file off the heavier blade until the fly no longer falls quickly back to the same position after being turned. This little adjustment will help the train to start running promptly with the minimum driving weight, so it is all to the good.

THE COUNTWHEEL

A missing countwheel is a common complaint with these clocks, but it is not difficult to replace – the major task is the wheel attached behind it, with its associated pinion, which has already been discussed. The countwheel will have been held by a lost spring clip of thin sheet brass and this also has to be replaced. It is most often triangular in shape with springy corners, but other shapes were also used (see Fig. 3). It is held in place with a pin through the stud on the back plate (as in the Burgess clock). Alternatively, a groove (often broken off) will be found in the end of the stud and this houses either a straight slip or a broken disc of brass with a slot to fit round the groove.

It is possible to have a countwheel cut by a firm advertising wheel-cutting services, but in fact wheels marked out and cut with a piercing saw by hand are perfectly satisfactory. Brass of about 1 mm thick is suitable. The size can be gauged from the position of the detent, which is usually horizontal when in a slot with the train locked. The depth of the slots is the difference between the 'high' and 'low' positions of the locking-piece with the train locked or running – the tip of the detent, which may be broken, should be long enough to reach the bottom of countwheel slots. Each slot represents one revolution of the hoopwheel and is 1/78th of the circumference of the countwheel. A suitably-sized blank can be covered with paper which is divided into segments of just under 5° with a protractor, or the circumference can be divided into 78 and measured round.

There is another way of doing this. Mount your brass blank on the countwheel stud with the pinion in place, and push the train round by hand. Every time the locking-piece drops into the hoop, there is a potential mark to be made on your blank under the countwheel detent; but of course you mark only at 1, 2, 3 etc falls of the locking-piece and detent until you have the blank fully marked out. In this procedure a countwheel slot is represented by one turn of the hoopwheel. The difficulty with this method is that the play of the gears may impede precise measurement; the difficulty with the other method is that exact measurement makes no allowance for play in the gears. You have to take your choice.

HAMMER SPRINGS AND STOPS

These parts are very subject to wear – and will function in a worn state. However, they can usually be re-surfaced much as in re-facing pallets as previously described.

BELLS AND BELL STANDARDS

It is not uncommon for bell standard and/or bell to be missing. Bells of various sizes are available from suppliers. The size required is gauged from the position of the hammer at rest and the top of the standard (or where it would be, if it is missing). The top is usually visible just above a square dial from the front. Thirty-hour clocks, particularly the earlier and posted ones, tend to use much larger bells than eight-day clocks, but remember that the hammer of a posted movement strikes the bell inside. Bells are almost invariably secured by a special nut. This can be made by tapping a thread into a square of brass about ⅛'' (3 mm) thick and lightly bevelling the edges. If unavoidable, the thread on the standard can be re-made to match.

There is considerable variation in the position and mounting of the bell standard. On the Burgess clock it is mounted below the pallet cock on the back plate and passes up through it. This (though not entirely convenient) is usual later practice. Other options are to one side of the pallet cock on the backplate, inside or outside, and outside the frontplate – the latter is a

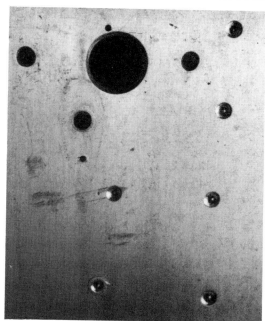

Fig. 55 Stain left by the missing bell standard

Fig. 56 Manufactured bell standard

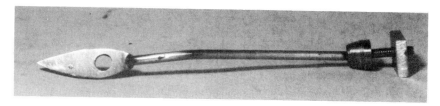

sign of an early eighteenth century or even seventeenth century movement. On posted movements the standard has a bent foot by which it is screwed to the frontplate. Blank standards are available for the backplate mountings and can be adapted for the front, but those for posted movements have to be fabricated by brazing pieces of steel together.

Where the standard is missing, the shape of the missing foot is usually discernible in the tarnish of the back (or top) plate (Fig. 55). In principle the feet need to be generous in size and fitted with at least one 'steady'. Sometimes the extreme tip of the foot was bent round to dig into the plate as a steady. Perhaps more often, steady pins were used. Either way, you will find a small hole close to the screw-hole for receiving the steady. The bell needs a small pillar or pedestal on which to rest, below the threaded section of the standard. This can be made separately, of round or square section, drilled and soldered into place. The standard made for the Scott movement is shown in Fig. 56. Standards of posted movements were usually made of square-sectioned steel. If you need to make one and do not have a lathe (and thus are confronted with a problem in making square metal round for the threaded part), it is possible to drill the end of the standard blind and insert a screw, of thread 2BA or thereabouts, fixing it with Loctite 601 retainer.

Assembly

With the repairs and reconditioning carried out, the striking works can be re-assembled for testing. For this it is simplest at first to temporarily omit the going wheels.

Striking mechanisms must be assembled in a certain way or the coincidences on which they depend will not occur reliably, and the resistance of hammer and spring may prevent the train from starting up. The train is always assembled in the locked position. The requirements are that when the train is locked, the countwheel detent must be in a countwheel slot (though this will of course be fitted afterwards), the hammer tail should not be resting on a hammer pin (ideally it should have just left one), and the warning wheel pin should be half a turn away from the warning-piece. This is the situation in Fig. 51a (although of course the hammer tail cannot be seen). The wheels tend to turn as their pivots are being located, so these settings are not always achievable in one attempt, but it is pointless to proceed to a trial run until the mechanism is disposed in this way. With some clocks, it helps to restrain the greatwheel (which tends to be pushed crooked by hammer and spring) with adhesive tape or thin wire while the other wheels and parts are being located. It is usually possible to relocate the greatwheel by removing only two plate pins and lifting the side of the plate. This convenience does not, of course, exist with a birdcage pillared movement.

Once the train is assembled and the plates fastened, attention turns to 'let off' and warning, the wheels being turned by hand. The critical factor here, whatever the type of mechanism, is that the warning piece must be raised into position ready to obstruct the warning pin when the train is released. If it is not, one or more blows will be struck at five (or more) minutes to the hour and the counting will go awry. The warning piece is raised by the lifting piece (of which it may be part) and linked to the locking piece. Adjustment depends on the type of mechanism (see Part IV). In later clocks, including the Burgess, no adjustment is needed unless gross distortion has occurred in the combined lifting/warning piece. In earlier clocks with the warning piece between plates, there is a connecting finger which is capable of adjustment by bending to advance or delay release of the train at warning. In all types, lifting or warning pieces are squared onto the extended end of either locking or warning piece arbor and it is *essential* that this attachment shows no play. The arbor's end may well be rounded and have to be re-squared. If you are lucky – as was the case with the Burgess movement's squared-on warning piece – wear will not be too severe and a blow from a hammer will tighten the square hole. However, previous punchings may have damaged the hole beyond further tightening, in which case the hole may need to be re-made with a collet of brass or steel freshly riveted into the enlarged hole in the attached piece. But, however it is achieved, this attachment must, when pinned, be really firm or the operation and timing of the striking will be unreliable. Exactly the same applies to the fit of the countwheel detent on its square at the back, though in later clocks this is often brazed to, or forged with, the arbor and locking piece, being shaped to pass through a hole in the backplate if it is solid.

Provided warning occurs correctly, the striking should now be satisfactory, since the locking mechanism has already been serviced. However, on trying the striking round through twelve hours, you might still find miscounting. The instinctive reaction here is always to suspect the countwheel – and indeed it may be the culprit *if new*. The only way to find out is to run repeated twelve-hour tests to discover whether or not the irregularity occurs always at the same place or places on the wheel. This is, admittedly, more difficult than it might sound since, once a miscount occurs, the mechanism is deranged and cannot easily be run backwards for a repeat run, but perseverance will eventually show if a section of the wheel is 'out'.

The above qualification *if new* is nonetheless very important. Countwheels undergo no wear in use and it is most improbable that there is a fault in an old longcase countwheel. Neither can any of your adjustments or repairs have affected it. There is no justification for attacking an old countwheel with a file and you are certain to regret it if you try to do so. The fault will be either in the locking, which has been reviewed, or, sometimes, in the coarse gearing which is used in this part of the clock. Because of the latter, it is quite common for a countwheel to work reliably in one position vis-a-vis the driving pinion, but not in other positions. Sometimes a pinion leaf will be punch-marked or bevelled-off, and this leaf has to be aligned with a small 'peep-hole', usually ringed, in the countwheel itself. Otherwise, it is worth trying several possible engagements – again, this can take some time, since the best engagement may well not coincide with the detent's being in a countwheel slot, i.e. with the beginning of a slot. The problem increases with low countwheel pinion counts; with a pinion of four there is much 'play' in the gears and the countwheel can take some time to position. If, after all, the detent persists in lodging twice in slots, it is worth considering adding to the width of the detent rather than narrowing the slots.

8   Rack Striking

Rack striking is the system most often used in eight-day longcase clocks. It was invented late in the seventeenth century to offer repeat striking on demand (e.g. at night) and rapidly became general in eight-day and bracket clocks, though was very seldom used in thirty-hour clocks. It was more expensive and less robust than countwheel striking, but it was reliable and it offered the repeat facility.

The working of the mechanism can be seen from Figs. 57 a–d, which show the striking of the Scott clock from just before striking (a), through warning (b) and running (c), and back to the locked position (d). The number of blows is controlled by a stepped cam (the 'snail'), which revolves with the hour wheel, and a toothed rack which falls upon it when the train is released. Evidently it will take longer, more blows, to raise the rack a short distance, as at 1.00 o'clock, than a long distance, at 10.00 o'clock for example. This raising of the rack is accomplished by a tooth or pallet (the 'gathering pallet') fitted to a train wheel, the 'locking wheel' (between plates). It is called the locking wheel because most often trains are locked by the catching of the pallet on a pin in the rack when the latter is fully gathered up – though there are other locking arrangements (see Part IV).

Rack striking is on the whole simpler to set up than countwheel striking. It is sometimes necessary to separate the assembled plates to ensure that the warning wheel has sufficient run or that the hammer tail is off the pin-wheel (as discussed in Chapter 7), but generally in rack striking such things look after themselves. However, the parts are easily damaged so that the gathering of the rack, tooth by tooth, does not correspond absolutely with the steps on the snail. Then there is trouble, for this correspondence is at the heart of the system. We will consider it later in the context of various repairs and replacements.

Gearing

The reasoning behind the gear train is based on the train's need always to be able to stop immediately after each blow. Thus the ratio of the pinion on the locking-wheel (the one with the gathering pallet) to the pin-wheel which drives it must be the same as the number of pins on the pin-wheel which lift the hammer – for it has to make one revolution for each blow of the hammer. Typically – as in the Scott clock – we have a locking wheel pinion of 7 and a pin-wheel of 56 teeth (ratio 1:8), with 8 lifting pins. Again, the ratio of the locking wheel to the warning wheel pinion (which is perhaps more likely to be missing) is always a whole number (here 7), so that the warning wheel always stops at the same distance from the warning piece. The whole Scott striking train is as follows:

Greatwheel	Pin-wheel	Locking wheel	Warning wheel	Fly
78	56	49	49	7
	7	7	7	

It will be noticed that the locking and warning wheels are of the same count; this is achieved by having a smaller tooth size (module) after the locking wheel. The ratio of fly to warning is important only for the speed of running – the pinions are sometimes only 6, which produces a high ratio and slower striking, typical of later clocks. If your clock has to have a wheel replaced, see Chapter 5.

The Rack and Snail

When the rack is fully gathered, the rack hook holds the first tooth against the tension of the rack spring, and the gathering pallet is located above the third or fourth tooth. Consequently there have to be more than twelve teeth on the rack, and in practice there are usually fourteen or fifteen. As the first three teeth are not gathered by the pallet, they do not need to be of full length – so long as the rack hook will hold them – and are sometimes graded in size to control additional striking at the quarters. However, this requires a modified snail and also an arrangement to silence one of the bells at the hour, making it too complex to be detailed here.

The size and spacing of the rack teeth are critical for the gathering pallet and rack hook, to enable reliable gathering, and for the snail, to ensure striking the correct number of hours. For the former, the pallet meets a tooth about to be gathered at a point half way, or a little less, down the straight face. Its turning should drag the shaped rack-hook up the following tooth, after which the hook falls into place (see below, 'Replacing the Gathering Pallet'). Failure in this sequence of events is not likely to be due to the rack overall, but individual teeth may need attention. As with an escapement, never file the flat (in fact, also radial) faces of the teeth, but only the curved backs. Individual teeth can be replaced as in gearwheels (see Chapter 5). Occasionally a pallet fails to lift teeth the required distance for proper movement of the rackhook, and then it is better

THE SEQUENCE OF RACK STRIKING

replaced than doctored.

The size and spacing of rack teeth are crucially related to the snail. Considered simply, the full movement of the rack tail at the snail, from one to twelve, is proportionately related to the length of the rack (starting from the first tooth actually used) from beginning to end. The relationship consists of identical *angles* made by the rack tail movement and by the rack movement – but of course, since the rack arm is longer than the rack tail, the actual *distance* travelled by the two is different. For the rack teeth, the angle of its movement is divided into twelve, each representing a tooth, and the additional two or three are added on. You can design and replace a rack on this basis, working with the circumference of a circle of which the rack arm to tooth-tip is a radius, and cutting the teeth by hand with a piercing saw. There is, however, much to be said here for having a specialist machine cut the teeth – which in fact is done as if the rack were a segment of a large, ratchet-toothed, gearwheel.

The rack tail may be missing or, more likely, broken or wrongly replaced. Solder is one give-away here, since the rack/rack-tail joint was always riveted, to facilitate final adjustment of angle. From what has been said of the rack, it will be seen that the exact length of the rack tail is vital to correct striking. Correcting it is certainly a repair which can be done at home.

The basic datum for rack-design is the straight-line distance from top to bottom of the snail, and that is where you start if you have to replace all parts, including the snail. Draw the triangle of the rack on paper, full size, with the stud's location at the bottom apex. On it superimpose the snail distance, exactly linking the two arms; the distance of this superimposed line from the stud is the length needed for the rack tail. The tail's shape is unimportant, but its effective length, from centre to engaging tip, is critical. If you have an altered rack tail and a clock which will not strike correctly, you can be virtually certain that the tail length is wrong. It is a very common problem. Cut the new tail from ½ mm brass and make its stud (which is where it is measured to end) with a slope which can 'jump' the steep edge of the snail should there be a failure to strike 12.00 o'clock. It is simplest to rivet it lightly in place before adjustment to working, then fasten with Loctite.

One step on the snail must correspond to one tooth on the rack.

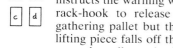

Fig. 57a Propelled by lifting pin and lifting piece, the warning lever instructs the warning wheel (in the hole) and shortly afterwards raises the rack-hook to release the rack; (b) the rack falls and releases the gathering pallet but the train is arrested by the warning; (c) when the lifting piece falls off the lifting pin, the warning is released and the train runs, the pallet gathering as many rack teeth (blows) as the snail permits; (d) when the rack is fully gathered, the pallet's tail lodges on the rack pin and the train is locked.

Therefore, rather than by measurement and machine-cutting, you can reconstruct a missing snail 'on the spot', if you have rack and tail. This is done by making a brass circular blank to the size indicated by the rack tail when the rack is fully gathered. Release one rack tooth, press the tail stud (if necessary, sharpened) into the blank and revolve it. This gives you a circle for the first tooth. Do the same with the other rack teeth in order. Then divide the blank into twelve and cut out the steps with the piercing saw. This method has the advantage of including any irregularities which there may be in the rack teeth. It can also be taken in reverse to gauge the spacing of rack teeth, using an improvised blank of rack and rack-tail, the dummy rack arm being given a point for marking metal below for the rack proper.

Replacing a Gathering Pallet

In the Scott clock the pallet was missing. This is very common, and the pallet's slipping off is the usual cause of that very vexatious phenomenon, 'continuous striking'. Sometimes there is a tiny pin through the arbor or it is threaded and a small nut put on, but most often gathering pallets are a push fit onto an arbor which may not even be tapered. Secondly, gathering pallets are subject to wear and become unreliable. It is not easy, nor is it really desirable, to build them up with slips of metal and solder. Making a new pallet is not difficult and does not call for any special tools, but it requires a certain amount of patient precision. If your pallet is missing, before you start to replace it make a thorough search of the case – they tend to lodge in cracks of the woodwork.

Pallet blanks can be bought or made, but to make them may be preferable for three reasons. Firstly, the bought ones need so much shaping that not much is gained. Secondly, their description is misleading – in fact 'left hand' means 'tail behind the rack' and 'right hand' means 'tail in front of the rack' but this is not easy to remember. Thirdly, the difficult square hole has still to be made in the bought ones.

The pallet has to be carved from solid and, as several measurements are critical, is best made on the big side and filed gradually to size.

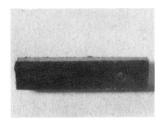  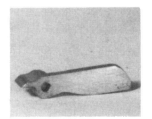

Figs. 58, 59 & 59a   Making a gathering pallet

Centre-punch and drill the hole as large as possible to save filing but still within the square's corners. Great care is needed in finely drilling steel to this depth and it is helpful to use turpentine as a lubricant. Fig. 58 shows the embryonic pallet at this stage – it has been kept on its stock for ease of handling.

The orientation of the square hole is important. Set up the train locked and ensure that the hammer has just left a hammer pin, then position the blank against the square while the pallet tail rests on the rack pin, and mark the outline of the square clearly on the pallet. In this case the hole needed to be in the 'diamond' position when locked. There is no short cut to making the square hole but it should not take too long if your drill was well chosen. Finish it with a fine square needle file, and then saw out the step so that the pallet tail is only about 1 mm thick (Fig. 59). The pallet face is radial from the hole. Cut straight down and remove a wedge, making sure that you have it the right way round, i.e. the radial face of the pallet to engage the radial face of rack teeth.

The rest consists of shaping the pallet in place. In order to clear the next tooth, the pallet will need to be less than half-a-tooth deep. It must, however, be long enough to move the rack till the rack hook jumps over the next tooth and goes half-way up the one after, before falling back into place. If the hook does not jump the tooth, the pallet is too short. If it jumps two teeth, the pallet is too long. The difference between the two is very small. Much the same judgement is needed, it may be said, with assessing wear on a pivot hole; and in fact it is hopeless trying to fit a new pallet if the square of the locking wheel arbor is loose (as it often is) in its hole. Finally, the tail is shaped so that it will lodge on the rack pin but not be too difficult to move; the rack must fall away readily (driven by its spring) when the rack-hook is raised. Sometimes it is made semi-circular with this in view; more often it is sloped, with the rack's locking pin resting just off the slope.

Adjustment

Unless there is obvious damage (as there was with the Scott rack, though not enough to affect its working), it is most improbable that there is anything seriously wrong with the rack when the striking is inaccurate; and it is inviting big trouble to start filing away at the teeth for a local improvement. A moment's reflection will confirm the latter, since any one tooth is used for more than one striking sequence; if you think to alter a tooth to correct, say, 8.00, you are liable to throw out 9.00 to 12.00, which may have been quite satisfactory.

Before you change anything, take the striking round several times and record every hour on a schedule, and then look for a pattern in the results. Then check the warning. When the lifting piece is slightly raised, the warning pin should run some half a turn and collide with the warning piece in the frontplate slot. If it misses the warning pin, with the clock starting to strike, it is likely that the long tail of the rack-hook needs to be bent upwards slightly, delaying the release of the train. Another seemingly baffling possibility is that the whole clock grinds to a halt at warning. This is because, by bad chance at assembly, the warning pin is directly above the warning piece when the train is at rest and has no 'run'; the only solution is to lift the plate and turn the warning wheel independently to a better position.

Then check the action of pallet and rack-hook before turning attention to the rack and snail. This action is best seen with the snail removed – you can then limit the area for investigation. Turning to rack and snail, if at the first step of the snail the pallet does not line up to gather one tooth (i.e. the rack does not fall far enough), the first presumption is that the riveted joint of rack and rack tail has worked loose. In this case the tail needs to be moved slightly downwards and the rivet made good or (though this is a last resort) carefully soldered. If, on the other hand, 2.00 is struck at the first step, obviously the reverse applies.

However, the commonest faults tend to have the symptom that the snail mysteriously seems to be too short or too long – 11.00 is as far as you can get or, if you reach 12.00, you cannot find 1.00 – something seems to be wrong in the middle. It is here that the temptation to file rack teeth *must* be resisted. These are rack tail problems; the essential correspondence between movement of the rack teeth and movement at the snail has been upset. Measure the tail exactly – from the edge of the centre of the sloped pin to the centre of the rack stud – and compare this with the criteria above. If the tail is too long, the rack will move too far, hardly perceptibly on the first tooth and cumulatively further as it proceeds. The clock can be made to strike 12.00 correctly, but at the cost of striking 2.00, or nearly so, at 1.00 o'clock. If the tail is too short, the reverse will apply and it may strike 12.00 twice. Sometimes a compromise can be reached in the angle of rack to rack tail, but it is more likely to be a case of replacing the rack tail as already described.

9 Date and Lunar Work

The Burgess clock has neither date nor moonwork, while the Scott clock has both. In this respect they are fairly typical of Victorian thirty-hour and eight-day longcase clocks. It is not uncommon to find a 'bought in' movement with a seconds escape wheel arbor but no provision for seconds on the dial; this is early 'mass production'. The Scott lunar work is incomplete – this again is par for the course. These accessories represent a considerable load for the weight to drive and, being extras, would tend to be discarded when the clock gave trouble. Also, as communications and lighting improved, the practical need for date and moon indicators became less great.

The Scott datework is of the simplest type – a pin (or nib) (visible in Fig. 48) on the hour-wheel turning a 31-toothed ratchet with the dates painted on its reverse and featured below the centre of the dial. (Other types are outlined in Part IV.) You would think that nothing much could go wrong here, but datework is in fact rather a murky area, especially at the lower end of the market.

Problem Datework

Nowadays datework (and moonwork) have an importance out of all proportion to their practical use. Although owners initially insist that their date indicators work, in a very short time most cannot be bothered to turn them on for the short months and in fact ignore them completely. Similarly, moonwork is seldom now used to identify (if necessary in advance, and weather permitting) a light night. The importance of such devices now is in their link with authenticity.

Quite often, as we have seen, in eight-day clocks there is a marriage between a movement and a brass dial which does not belong. The brass dial has been thought more appealing and more valuable – brass dials did indeed exist long before painted dials. However, brass and painted dials were associated with different day-of-the-month mechanisms (see Park IV). The brass dial usually had a small square aperture low on the dial, displaying a number from a large (appr. 0.7'', 180 mm) brass ratchet-toothed ring mounted on two rollers or pulleys, and a retaining hook, behind the dial. This ring was moved every twenty-four hours by an upright 'flag' finger fixed to a wheel (the 'twenty-four-hour wheel') meshing with the hour motion wheel and geared with it 1:2. (This wheel was mounted on a stud on the frontplate and meshed in fact with a large brass 'pinion' situated just below the snail fixed to the hour pipe.) The painted dial, on the other hand, more often used a small sixty-two-toothed ratchet, simply operated twice in twenty-four hours by the pin on the hour wheel. As mentioned, the aperture was then close to the centre. The numbers were painted on the painted dial's ratchet and engraved on the brass dial's ring.

In changing from painted to brass dial for a 'marriage', there would arise the problem that the attractive brass dial selected would have (or have had) a ring quite incompatible with a movement equipped for a painted dial. Moreover, its aperture would be in the wrong place. The change, therefore, with these common types of movement inevitably involved a degree of vandalism. The commonest solution was to fix the brass dial's ring at one date, or to solder a plaque with one date number showing permanently in the dial aperture (as was done also when a ring was lost or discarded). Although it was not strictly impossible to convert such a movement by fitting a new twenty-four-hour wheel and flag, together with a driving 'pinion' on the hour pipe, the amount of work might not be justified by the value of the new ensemble, particularly if a new ring had to be made by the engraver. Moreover, where – as is often the case – the brass dial's pillars had been moved to fit the movement, there might be no room for a 'brass' type of date ring at all, and replacing with wheels and solid ratchet (to operate the original low aperture by the 'hour wheel pin' method) would require further alteration even less likely to be worthwhile.

The moral is: be very wary of datework which is fixed or has parts missing, or accept the obvious alteration as a fact of the clock's history and do not compound the flaw by making further alterations. Altered datework often indicates a 'marriage', and its correction, if only to have it up and going, will involve further departures from authenticity. Moreover, you probably would not be able to handle it yourself.

Repairing Datework

There are so many potential problems of clearance in the small space between frontplate and dial that it is always best in this sort of work to make an accurate full-sized drawing of the environs.

First, simple datework on a painted dial. The rough size of a missing disc will be obvious from the dial. Its exact size is found from the pin or finger attached to the hour wheel; this should engage half-way, or a little less, down a ratchet tooth. If you have a friend with a lathe or wheel-cutting machine, he or she can cut you sixty-two nice even ratchet teeth. But, if not, it is possible to use angles of 5.8° round the circle and cut the teeth with a piercing saw. Absolute accuracy is not essential here. Make the disc of 1 mm brass and paint it with acrylic. In all of this, do be careful of direction. The disc and numbers move anti-clockwise. It is all too easy to number clockwise in error. A decent effect can be had for the numbers using Lettraset or similar dry transfers, followed by a stabilizing coat of lacquer. This will not fool the expert, but if you are in the business of fooling experts it would be better to have the job done by an experienced specialist anyway.

As has already been said, the length of the operating pin is critical. To find it will take some experiment. Similarly with the pin's angle at the hour pipe, the radius of the circle which the pin describes depends on this angle. If it engages too deeply with the ratchet, more than half a day's division will be moved, and conversely if it is set too shallow. In fact, the circle described by the pin corresponds nearly with a circle of which the back of the ratchet tooth forms part. These ratchets usually but not always have a restraining pawl which is simply a strip of brass soldered or screwed to the falseplate. Arrange it so that the divisions of the ratchet coincide with the dial aperture and the registered date is in the middle.

Brass dial datework is more difficult to replace. As the internally-toothed date ring must be engraved (any other method is offensive on a brass dial) it may be possible to have the engraver cut the ring at the same time. Alternatively, a specialist wheel cutter will do it. The centres of these rings are seldom the centres of their dials, but can be found by copying the positions of rollers and retaining hook (at the top, in the dial back) onto paper and then using a pair of compasses. The depth of the ring obviously depends on the extent of the 'flag' finger which moves it, and you may have a little scope if this is missing. If fitting a new flag, again an accurate drawing of the area is essential, and here you have to be careful not to confuse back and front views (and rotation directions). The flag must clear the neighbouring winding-square and miss the highest step of the striking snail, a cut-out (surprisingly big) being usual for the latter purpose (see Part IV). For the flag, do not use too thin metal; about 2 mm thick is needed for a good rivet into the twenty-four-hour wheel. Again, make the flag initially too big, cutting it down by experiment.

The twenty-four-hour wheel has twice the number of teeth which are on the hour wheel 'pinion', which is less likely to be missing. If you have to replace this wheel, offer the hour wheel to the supplier and indicate the diameter required, i.e. twice the distance from the stud (or hole for it) to the meshing point. Occasional suppliers stock a range of these wheels, in various sizes and counts, but cutting one specially is not a difficult job and should not be expensive.

Moon Phases – General

The age of the moon was important information before the era of artificial light. So far as domestic clocks are concerned, the establishment of the arched dial early in the eighteenth century was correspondingly a boon, and the space of the arch was often used for showing the state of the moon. Nor did makers neglect the magnificent decorative potential of richly coloured moon phases on a brass and silvered dial. Similar designs on painted dials also have their more intimate charm, and indeed it seems likely that the lovely moonscapes of brass dials were one impulse towards complete painted dials in the later eighteenth century. As most cheap thirty-hour clocks continued to have square dials, moon phase indication is less common on them, but even here many more costly ones were made complete with moon data and, for fishing localities, local tides could be shown on the same scale, though this would have needed special co-operation with the dial writer. With the square dials, the additional information could be given either by further hands or by discs moving behind apertures.

There is a great variety of devices to indicate the moon's age, more or less accurately. (Some of the commonest are shown in Part IV.) For this purpose the moon was taken to 'die' after 29½ days, the lunar month being more exactly 29.53 days. In this cycle the moon waxes from new to full, and wanes from full to old; the full moon is the half-way point, the new moon is no moon, just a background. None of the regular 'clock' moon devices gives a very close picture of the moon as its phases are actually observed. For reference you may find helpful a simple summary of the moon's apparent behaviour, such as that in a children's book by H. Couper and N. Herbert, *The Moon* (Franklin Woods, 1986).

The Scott clock has the commonest form of lunar phase indication in the dial arch. This is of the two-cycle type; the big disc represents two complete cycles of lunar phases and rotates in fifty-nine days. Because in this type the 118-toothed ratchet disc is worked from the hour wheel (by the same pin or nib which operates day-of-the-month), there is a spatial problem: a disc to reach down to this pin would be enormous and would foul the dial feet (as some discs nearly do) and seconds hand arbor.

In different types this space is filled either by a wheel or, as here, by some sort of 'deer's foot lever' which drives the ratchet disc. The lever consists of a fork and a freely riding pallet. In this case the lever was missing, but the stud and a stop pin for it were still attached to the back of the dial. (With eight-day clocks having painted dials, the stud and return springs were often mounted on the falseplate rather than the dial.) The lever should be freely pivoted and the pallet have a large tail whose weight ensures that the pallet is always engaged with the ratchet teeth.

Where people were prepared to dispense with a seconds hand, lunar phases (one cycle) could be put in that hand's usual position above the centre, a fifty-nine-toothed ratchet disc being driven exactly as the date disc below the centre. The display was a rounded aperture below 12.00 o'clock and there was of course no need for a lever. This is very common in work from Lancashire and Yorkshire and may be called a 'penny' moon in its various forms.

Repairing Arch Moon Phase Mechanism

Before making any parts for this type of mechanism, it is essential to do what can be done (sometimes, alas, not much) to true the axis of the disc. These discs are so large that the slightest looseness in their mounting or

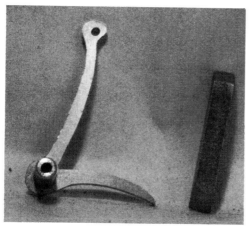

bending of the stud produces so much play at the ratchet teeth that there is no hope for any pallet to engage. Often the disc's pipe is loose at the base; it may be possible to strengthen it with washers and Superglue or epoxy adhesive. A stronger job can be made if this sort of work is done before the disc's paintwork is restored. As has been seen, it may not worry the owner much or for long (even if the owner is in fact you), but a disc which does not revolve full circle because it is untrue is not

Fig. 60   'Deer's foot' lever for driving moonwork

acceptable craftsmanship. Some wobble or 'shake', of course, is inevitable, and the pallet has to be thick enough to accommodate that. As for the Scott clock, the stud thread was partially stripped but it was possible to stabilize the stud with Loctite. The pipe was a serviceable fit.

Restoring the Scott mechanism involved first making an accurate full-sized drawing of the back of the dial and so measuring the spaces able to be filled between moon disc, stud and hourwheel pin. Lever and pallet were then sketched in, noting that the disc is *driven* by the hourwheel but *returned* by a spring, and that the pallet must not be placed too close to the disc when drawing, since in practice such a position will lead to problems in clearing the disc teeth. The parts were first drawn as straight lines and then fleshed in with the aid of stencil French curves.

The lever was made of ½ mm brass and fitted with a pipe made from bushing tube; the hole was broached out from one direction, which imparted the taper appropriate to the existing stud (Fig. 60 – lever and blank for pallet). It is desirable, although not essential, for the pallet to be of steel and it should be of a good thickness, to cover any wobble in the disc.

In shaping the pallet, it is as well to try it, undrilled and unfinished, in the lever's 'backward' position, to establish the precise place for the pallet hole. Otherwise, much time can be wasted in polishing and adjusting, only to discover that the pallet is slightly too long or too short. Finally, the lever requires a pin or bent edge to catch the pallet tail and hold it against the driving pressure on the pallet itself (here it must be admitted that an edge was introduced at a late stage because it had been overlooked that the lever's metal was too thin to support a pin), and the return spring is made from thin brass, hammered to harden it (Fig. 61 – the hooked spring on the left here is for the day-of-the-month ratchet). Fig. 62 shows the moon mechanism restored.

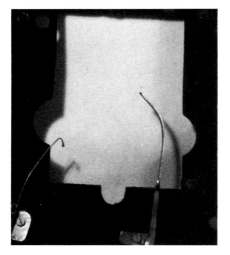

Fig. 61   Lever return spring

Fig.   62   Scott   moon   mechanism restored

10   Hands and Dials

Although restoration in this area may appeal to those not so mechanically-minded, it would be an error to regard it in any way as a soft or easy option. In the past, the making of hands and dials was carried out largely by specialist craftsmen. Depending on the clock's age and potential value, one should never be ashamed to hand this work to an expert if not reasonably confident of success. This applies particularly to painted dials, whose restoration prospects can be ruined by improper cleaning, painting or lacquering. It is respect for the original which must decide the issue. There are a number of dial-restorers advertised in the specialist magazines. The easiest way to distinguish between them is to request 'before and after' photographs of work which they have carried out, unless, of course, you are able to visit and form your own judgement. It is a matter of assessing not only the calibre of workmanship but also the style and character of work which each restorer tends to produce.

Hands

One solution to broken or missing hands is to look through the catalogues of suppliers until something suitable is found. There are published surveys of the development of clock hands, and several authoritative books on different types of clocks have a wealth of photographic information. So finding an appropriate and even correct pattern may not be very difficult.

However, there is a large selection of hands from suppliers which, while right in style and possibly adequate in size, will nonetheless mar otherwise well-restored pieces. Most of them are stamped from sheet-metal, including aluminium, and sprayed to colour. Thicker steel hands, properly blued, can be obtained but they are expensive and may not be of the exact size required. Nineteenth century hands can often be replaced cheaply from these sources, however, leaving you only to fit and pierce suitable collets where necessary – the chapter rings tend to be of standard sizes.

EXAMPLE BRASS HANDS

Both the example clocks had, or had had, brass hands. The older blued steel hands are also found with painted dials, however, dating in general

Fig. 63   Burgess hands as received

from the eighteenth century and less commonly from the nineteenth.

The Burgess hands (Fig. 63) were judged not to be original, but they might have been copies of the original; they are in a well-known, although not especially common, Victorian pattern. Replacements of this pattern could not be located, and in fact the copy hands were felt to be good enough to be worth saving. In their received state they were very heavy in appearance and seemed to mask the dial, so it was decided to lighten and relieve them. ('Relieving' refers to the notches and other filings which tend to turn flat sheet-metal into a three-dimensional object. It is an important aspect of antique hands.)

In this case, one cause of the heaviness was that all the characteristic holes had been drilled to the same size, so these were enlarged towards the boss to produce a tapered effect and the angles were filed away to make the outlines stand out. Brass hands often have pressed indentations (similar to earlier relieving) across them by way of ornament, but this has to harmonize with the punched work and nothing was added in this respect. The fitting of the hands did not require attention. The finished pair is seen in Fig. 64.

The Scott clock also had brass hands, but the surviving hour hand (Fig. 65), which had been repaired with a soldered brass bridge, was weak

Fig. 64   Burgess hands modified

Fig. 65   Damaged hour hand of Scott clock

and the seconds, minute and date hands were missing and had to be replaced anyway, so it was decided to buy a complete set of similar style (Fig. 66). The surfaces of these were already well polished and lacquered, but the edges needed smoothing and, of course, had to be fitted, which will be discussed shortly.

STEEL HANDS – REPAIRING AND MAKING

Steel hands to be repaired must be silver-soldered – soft solder is not strong enough. Sometimes a joint can be reinforced with a slip of steel behind. If you are not familiar with hard-soldering, try it first on scrap metal, which must be thoroughly cleaned with emery. Apply the recommended flux to both surfaces and bring them to red heat. They are then brought touching or almost touching, and the stick of solder just tipped on the join, when the solder should flow in. If it does not, you may have insufficient flux, but more probably the metal was not clean enough to start with. The heat from a butane canister is quite adequate for clock repairs.

If an original set of hands can be saved by repair, so much the better, but often one or more hands have to be replaced. There is a wide range of hands available, both in quality and design. Where full replacement is necessary, styles can be identified from some of the books listed under Further Reading (Cescinsky and Webster are the classic source). However, it often is the case that either the pattern or the size is available, but not both. You then have to consider making your own.

Here the amateur is at an advantage. The problem is less in the materials or the skill than in the time which it takes to cut and finish a good hand – which helps to explain the high prices of craftsman-made hands on the market. You need some eight hours to make a steel hour hand. The major benefit, of course, is that hands of your own make can be of a preferred pattern and of exact size – the minute hand reaching just to the outer chapter ring and the hour hand not short of the hour ring.

By way of materials you need mild steel of between 1–2 mm ($\frac{1}{16}$″) thick. This can be scrap or bought specially, 'Gauge plate' makes a nice hand but is very hard to work. The prime requirement is that the metal will blue well; it is wise to test a corner in a flame for this, because several hours making a hand only to find that it must be blued with lacquer is disappointing to say the least. If it rusts, it will blue. In fact old, slightly rusted metal can be very good for hands.

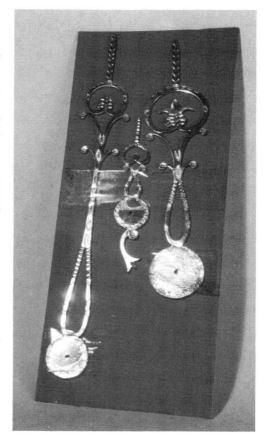

Fig. 66   Replacement brass hands

A little should be added to what has been said earlier about the tool for this job. Money is well spent on the best quality of piercing saw; cheap ones with poor screws for fixing blades, and with small throats (less than, say, 4″, 100 mm) are not conducive to good work. For cutting this way (i.e. up and down) the blade is fitted with the teeth pointing downwards. A good sawing table is produced by Chronos Ltd. Quite an acceptable one can be made at home from 1″ wood sawn into a Vee and with a block screwed to the back for gripping in a vice (see the table illustrated in Chapter 15). It is very difficult to do this work without such a table or with one that flexes.

Accept at the outset that you are going to break blades, and have a good supply to hand. They blunt quite quickly when cutting steel. Sawing with a blunt blade is frustrating and blunt blades are prone to break. Generally speaking, one may err towards too coarse a blade in the early stages, to minimize breakage; but in fact the finer blade will move more easily, removing less metal, snag less and be more accurate in following a line.

Whether you mark the metal direct or stick a paper pattern to it, a full-sized drawing on paper should be made. This can be used to ensure a symmetrical hand; draw a whole hand, fold the paper down the middle and, selecting the better side, cut it out in double thickness. Copy or carbon the internal design, and try the pattern in place on the dial before starting to cut metal.

At sharp angles, and tight curves as well if you like, drill a small hole for

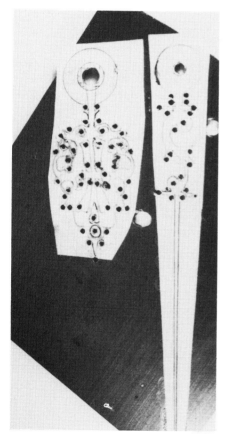

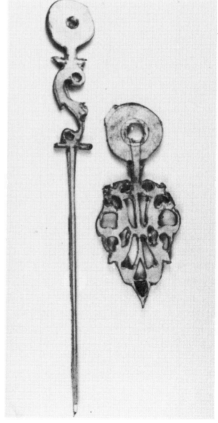

Fig. 67   Cutting out a steel hand

Fig. 68   Steel hands roughed out

the blade. With practice, you will find that fewer of these holes are needed. Hands at this stage are shown in Fig. 67.

There is a good general rule to do the 'internal' work first while there is still a substantial body of metal to hold on the sawing table. This inside fretwork includes the mounting circle or square, at least of the hour hand; it is much easier to cut with a saw than to drill and file square holes.

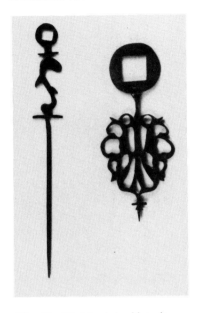

When sawing steel it can be helpful to pass the blade between oiled or turpentined fingers before starting. You will find that working with a piercing saw is a matter of practice. Sawing should be a relaxed and easy rhythm, not violent and hasty jerks. Try to use most of the blade in a stroke, rather than a small part of it. Above all, keep the work firmly held and never twist the blade. You can turn the blade – in practice one usually turns the work – through surprisingly sharp angles so long as you maintain the sawing motion while doing so. The difficulty of entering a new hole, or an edge, can be eased by using the blade in reverse, like a file. As you progress, you will be able to come closer to the marked line, but be wary; a wide cut can be filed down but a close cut cannot be remedied. The hands are shown cut out in Fig. 68.

Fig. 69   Finished steel hands

Part of the appeal of good old steel hands lies in the balance between overall solidity and fine internal detail. Often they are virtually three-dimensional – in the eighteenth century there was a tendency for the minute 'hand' actually to delineate a hand and index, while later this reference was lost. When simply sawn and tidied up, your hand will be a little disappointing, as it still has to be relieved. This is done partly by making a cleft mark, with saw and triangular file, extending sharp angles inwards so that they are sloping and widening towards the outside edge from a narrow crack inside. It was not used at every apex but is very common at the start of curves, particularly the bows of the hour hand. Another decoration was line-marking, a survival from the lantern-clock and single-handed era; it was common to mark the tail of a single hand with two or three punched lines straight across the tip. This appears also on the tips of hands or where the index joins the boss, or it is applied as a form of shading to bulb-like shapes. Finally, a taper in thickness over the whole length of minute hands is common, and also over the points of hour hands. Some of these devices were added to the hands whose progress we have been following (see Fig. 69).

BLUEING STEEL HANDS

The quality of the blueing greatly affects the overall impression. Before blueing by any method, you must bring the work up to a bright finish. Blueing with heat is traditional and, at its best, superb, but it is somewhat chancy. Blueing salts are simply a means of distributing the heat for an even colour. Blue enamel is an admission of defeat and seldom looks right, but it does have a use for touching in silver-soldered joints. Rubbing with gun blueing paste is simple and reliable, though it produces a less good colour than blueing with heat.

To blue with heat, the hand is laid on a brass plate or, better still, a bed of brass filings (simply to distribute the heat through an uneven mass) and heated until dark blue. Care is needed to obtain an even blue – the thin tip turns blue first, then loses its colour. The blued metal will also lose its colour if over-heated. The hand is then plunged into water (some prefer salt water), dried and rubbed with oil. Salts are heated to boiling point, then let drop a little and the hand is immersed until it reaches the desired colour. For handling, it is simplest to use a length of wire bent round the boss. The salts can be left to harden when cold, then used on future occasions. They are poisonous and dangerous, producing a violent reaction if touched with water. Because of this – but also as a general rule to any method – an unsatisfactory hand should not be immediately re-treated but instead dried, polished back to its natural colour and then submitted to the whole process again. However they are blued, steel hands can be given a coat of lacquer, which further enhances their finish as well as protecting them.

FITTING HANDS

The difficulties of fitting clock hands can easily be under-estimated. It can take a long time and involve considerable risks to what may be expensive or valuable hands.

Seconds hands may be supplied without pipes. New pipes are obtainable as 0.5 mm 'bushing wire' (fine tube) and can be either turned down to fit an enlarged hole in the hand (when it is riveted on) or soft-soldered in place. Both methods were used in new clocks – soldering was adopted here on the assumption that a lathe was not available. Cut the pipe to length with the dial in place, assuming it goes back to 1 cm of the frontplate, then drill it out for the arbor. The hole is finished with a broach to give it a taper. The hand and pipe are then cleaned off with emery, brought to a good heat and tinned with solder, the pipe being held up by a 'third hand' gadget or some convenient object. The two can then be brought together and touched with the hot iron (used, instead of a flame, to preserve the hand's finish), when they will fuse. The solder-filled hole can be touched in with gold paint or pen. Fig. 70 shows the mounted Scott seconds hand.

Fig. 70 Fitted brass seconds hand

The problem with both main hands is safe enlargement of the holes; the hands are difficult to hold and there is serious risk of their being bent or broken during drilling. It is best to drill no more than half the diameter and then to laboriously broach and file the rest. The hour hand of the Scott clock has a round pipe and a retaining screw; this is the commonest fitting. As already mentioned in Chapter 4, alternatives are a locating pin instead of the screw, or a square-ended pipe. In these cases the hands are either pressed on or pinned through the corners of the square in front of the hand. Less often an hour hand is held by an open spring washer pressed into a ring slot in the pipe. The position for the hole for pin and screw is

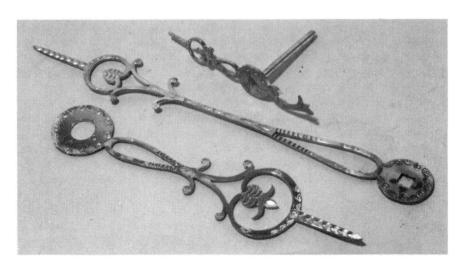

Fig. 71   Completed brass hands

important, being governed by the snail which is fixed to this pipe; obviously the hand must point to 12.00 when the appropriate snail section is struck by the rack tail. The position is normally below where the hand joins the boss (although, as can be seen in Fig. 65, there has been alteration here where someone has reversed the position of snail and hand-screw). The retaining screw selected must be a good fit and, if necessary, the hole can be re-tapped to match. (The new Scott hand is shown in Fig. 71.)

The hole in the minute hand can be set square or as a diamond to the hand; either way, it will be matched to the hour by turning the cannon pinion relative to the minute wheel. Start the square by enlarging it to fit the tip of the arbor and then square it by filing to fit the pipe. Take time and trouble here, for loose or punched-up holes in minute hands are a great nuisance.

Minute hands on most clocks are held in place by a pin through their arbor tip. The fitting of this pin requires a certain care and is described in Chapter 11. On some late provincial clocks without a centre arbor the minute hand pipe is threaded and a large-headed screw replaces the original pin. This is perhaps less attractive to look at but is a very practical arrangement. It is quite common for the centre arbor to have been broken off at the pin-hole near its tip. This simple but serious trouble poses quite a problem for the amateur and, unless you have a lathe, it will probably be best to have a craftsman file the end square, fit a plug and drill a new hole. Because the hand is pressed on against the bowspring, there is very little hope of, for example, wiring it on to the stub without a taper pin.

Brass Dials

The dial plate and spandrels (corner-pieces) can be cleaned in the same way as the movement, though it is not usual to clean brightly the backs of dial plates. If you do not wish to re-wax the silvered chapter ring, do not immerse it – the cleaning solution removes all the wax.

Silvering and re-waxing are quite feasible for amateurs and will be outlined for the derelict thirty-hour ring illustrated in Fig. 72, which was in as sad a state as you are ever likely to meet, being solid grey and virtually illegible. When cleaned it was found to be of the early or middle eighteenth century, extremely plain and with diamond marks between the entries. This tends to suggest that it is of Quaker origin.

The ring was first cleaned in the solution and then rinsed and brushed off with a soft hand brush. The remains of the old wax could then be scraped out. At this stage a scrubbing board was introduced. This is simply a thick square or rectangular board in which holes can be made for the ring's feet and into which a screw can be driven to be the centre of the ring's circle (Fig. 73). To this screw is attached a cord with a large cork or piece of cork sanding-block fixed to it in such a way that the block is held on course

Fig. 72   A chapter ring before restoration

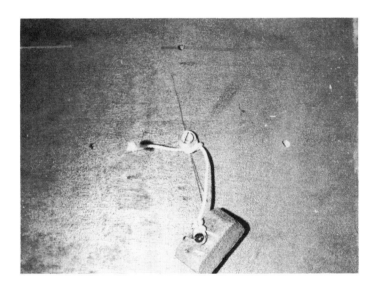

Fig. 73   Dial scrubbing board

round the chapter ring and various grades of 'wet and dry' paper can be applied in circular motion. These are used wet (to stop them clogging), and it is convenient if the board can be installed in a sink or basin.

Since most extant originals have been re-silvered several times in their life-time, it is not easy to know what was the typical first finish. One finds very few 'unsilvered' brass dials which do not (on inspection) show evidence of having been silvered at some time in their lives. However it does seem likely that there will have been some left unfinished in this way, and whether or not you now silver them is really a matter of personal preference. Whether or not there was a circular grain, and how deep it was, has also been much discussed, and no doubt practice varied widely. One can only leave the matter to personal taste and advise against imposing a very heavy grain. Clearly as little metal as possible should be removed, and it may be preferable to leave surface defects rather than to sand down to complete flatness all over. In this case there were irregular grazes and grains and a paper was selected to give a fine overall grain. The edges were treated with similar paper – it is important to the final appearance that chapter ring edges receive the same treatment as the flat surface.

After the ring had been washed, waxing was begun. This can be done over a camping stove or other source of gentle heat, resting the ring on a metal sheet with holes for the feet. A rag and many pieces of card about $2'' \times 1''$ (50 mm × 25 mm) are needed. The ring is warmed until the stick of wax will just melt, and this is then applied to the engraving. While excessive wax is a nuisance, it is essential to cover everything with a thin coating at this stage. The ring is kept warm but not sufficient to burn the wax, which is then scraped off as far as possible with the edges of card. The less wax which remains outside the engraving the better because, when set, it is very difficult to remove. Sometimes pieces of engraving are very shallow and may need to be touched up with fresh wax when the main application has been reduced with the cards. (Probably they are shallow because they have been taken back and resilvered so many times before.) Fig. 74 shows the wax applied at this stage.

The ring is now immersed in water and the 'spare' wax removed with 'wet and dry' paper used wet. Our ancestors used an abrasive like pumice powder, but this paper is now by far the best means. A grade is needed which will not impose further grain, and of course it must be applied round the dial or contradictory scratches will result. You must be able to bridge the flat surfaces, and for this a big cork again is useful as a sanding block. Again also there will be wax on the edges, and they should not be forgotten. Make no mistake – this job is hard graft! The result looks as in Fig. 75. Unwanted marks from the papering can be taken out with the abrasive block.

The final process is silvering and lacquering. You can obtain silvering

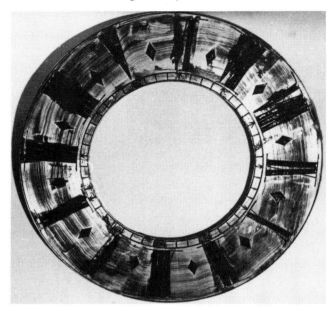

Fig. 74   Ring after waxing

Fig. 75   Ring after level sanding

powder (silver chloride) all ready for use. With the ring wet, this is applied thickly, rubbing it in with a thumb or soft rag until the surface takes on a muddy appearance. The surface is brightened by rubbing in either finishing powder or a paste of household Cream of Tartar and water. The latter seems no less satisfactory than commercial powders and can also be used to brighten up a ring which one does not wish to re-silver in full. (Sometimes, for example, yellow streaks appear after a few days, and Tartar paste will remove them without re-silvering, provided that methylated spirits have been used to shift any lacquer.) Do not be stingy with either silvering or finishing powder – go over the ring several times with abundant powder. The finishing paste is rubbed in until the silvered metal is a dull white. At this point it is washed and should come out bright (Fig. 76). It is then lacquered, using a clear lacquer on cotton wool and being careful that the surface is not touched by the hands. It is best to apply the lacquer with the ring held at an angle to a good light – it is extremely easy to put on an incomplete coat, and this defect will show itself in a few days.

Fig. 76   Finished ring

Painted Dials

The dial plays a major part in most people's assessment of a cased clock. Its condition and finish are quite as important as those of the mechanism. Therefore study the dial carefully before deciding what is to be done and who is to do it. How far is it worn or damaged, and how sharp and bright do you want it? There hardly ever seems to be a case for retaining untouched more or less illegible figures (though it is surprising what people will tolerate in the cause of 'looking old'), but retention of original decoration and coloured work is another matter.

Most restorers, naturally, produce a comparatively bright and clear dial, with detail (including the signature) restored or conjectured. Up to a point you can give instructions such as not to 'over-restore', but such matters are subjective. It does often make sense to have a really battered dial professionally restored. On the other hand, if the damage is not too great – particularly if not too much is actually missing – a good deal can be done by a careful owner, who then has some control over the brightness of the result. Again, a dial may be generally sound but have small local blemishes which can be remedied at home. However, it has to be accepted that amateur-restored dials tend to be a little dull and wobbly because of lack of experience and confidence, and much-crazed dials, with chips and rust as well, are probably better handled professionally.

The market for tools and materials is improving all the time so far as home restoration is concerned. A very wide range of paints is available as well as graded pens and brushes. The originals used some sort of oil-based

Fig. 77   Burgess painted dial before restoration

paints, but oils take practice to use well and they also take a long time to stabilize. It is safer to opt for acrylic paints, which dry in a few minutes and dissolve slowly in water, so that they are easily thinned in a palette and can be toned down or removed in a crisis. India ink is best for writing. French polish and black dye were used on later dials and are more durable, but they are much more difficult to handle. While there are black ink pens with graduated synthetic tips, they are not recommended – spirit pens in particular – because they are indelible and make life very difficult for future restorers. It is worth remembering that the better you do your job the more likely it is that the dial will be restored in many years to come!

The Example Dials

The Burgess dial (Fig. 77) was faded and some of the black work was crazed, but all the outlines seemed visible apart from the signature and town. These were brought out by ultra-violet light and pencilled in. Apart from slight chippings at the edge, the paint backing was undamaged. This is somewhat unusual – filling and matching hollows and cracks is a common part of dial restoration. There were cracks around the dial feet but these

Fig. 78 Scott painted dial before restoration

Fig. 79 Scott dial after professional restoration

were not very bad. These round marks are very common blemishes.

The back of the dial is painted with red lead paint and the dial feet are turned brass. Both back and feet were dirty and discoloured. This is usual; it is traditional not to clean these areas, although the feet can be brightened up. Sometimes the back will reveal signatures and dates, but there were no such markings here.

It was decided, all in all, to restore this dial in house. The Scott dial, however, was another matter (Fig. 78), being much more decorative with sharper detail, probably brighter colours, many crazes, the usual bare dial foot patches and some deeper damage. It was decided to have this dial restored, as shown in Fig. 79.

CLEANING AND FILLING

The first thing to do when restoring a painted dial is to clean it and here, of course, there is the very great danger that you will find some matter unstable. It is essential to proceed by steps from the gentler to the harsher cleaners and solvents. A reasonable sequence is window-cleaner, through graded metal polishes (wadding, liquid, then paste), to more abrasive compounds used in cleaning car cellulose, the latter being used sparingly indeed. White spirit can be used, but methylated spirit and real turpentine dissolve the paint. Try every cleaner on a scrap of plain outside edge and a tiny piece of writing before wading in.

There were no chips or serious cracks on the Burgess dial but, where there are, they can be filled now, after cleaning. For this a clear epoxy resin is used, mixed with powdered chalk. It is then sanded down with fine *clean* sandpaper and painted with lacquer to restore the glaze. Ceramic white tile adhesive is a useful alternative to the resin filler. The real problem, of course, is to match the background tint. For this, considerable experiment is required and ideally the resultant colour is mixed in with the filler, though it can be applied afterwards. A somewhat surprising constituent of the background colour is nearly always the shade yellow ochre, and this is added to the palette until the desired shade is reached, bearing in mind (if you included it in the filler) that it can be touched up with the brush before lacquering. The true colour is not apparent until the mix has thoroughly dried, so take time to experiment in a 'safe' place, preferably on scrap material.

DIAL-WRITING – THE BURGESS DIAL

The cleaned dial is now dried and polished with a dry cloth and attention turned to the missing material – such as could be identified. There was a question-mark over dial rings, and parts of figures were obviously missing, but these do not need to be done at this stage. The clear defect was signature and town. However, better missing than recently inked in and possibly inauthentic. Using the ultra-violet light in a dark room, the outlines of the broad-nibbed missing writing – which could be discerned, though not read, by holding the surface up horizontally to daylight – were put in with a soft pencil. All the writing would be done in this 'profile' way; for one thing, it is easily altered and, for another, inks do not always flow well on dial surfaces and the use of broad nibs can be difficult. The pencilled outlines are just visible in Fig. 80. It is in fact clear from worn dials that much of the dial writing was originally done in 'outline' form.

Fig. 80 Pencilled markings for restoring Burgess signature, made under ultra-violet light

In starting actual painting, it is usual to tackle the writing first and one may work broadly from the centre outwards, mixing that with 'top to bottom'. The object is, of course, to have your working arm crossing newly painted work as little as possible. The Burgess inscription was taken first, using a 0.1 mm 'tube' (Rotring-type) pen and slightly diluted India ink. It is helpful to add a couple of drops of washing-up liquid or glycerine to the ink bottle; this assists flow. It is very trying to be scribing along when all of a sudden the loaded pen refuses to leave a mark.

After the pencilled outlines had been inked in – and corrected, in a better light than when they were drawn – the enclosed area was blackened with a medium italic-nibbed pen. In outlining, although accuracy is important, painstaking exactness can spoil the effect, producing a wavering line rather than a confident rhythm, so it is necessary to work with some speed (knowing that the ink is not indelible). If you can persuade an edged or flexible pointed pen to flow, this is well worth while in imitating original calligraphic shapes. Some prefer to use a brush. A 'mapping pen' nib is also useful for fine lines. One of the difficulties is the apparent awful finality of it all – suppose a blodge descends the first time you apply the pen. To minimise the likelihood of mistakes, it is helpful to have a piece of smooth scrap metal alongside on which to run the nibs in. But, provided you use India ink, mistakes should not be disastrous.

The inscription was done freehand, but the writing proper – the chapter rings and figures – must be done entirely with ruler and compasses. First of all it is necessary to establish the true centre of the rings, which applies also to the numerals. This may not be the centre of the dial hole and in any case the hole may be worn – this one was oval, no doubt due to the drag of the dial over the years and adjustments made for it. Plug the hole with cork or wood and experiment with a pencil in the compasses. These may be extended 'beam' compasses, or you can make a serviceable instrument from a strip of wood or metal using a screw to grip the pencil and a sharpened screw moving in a slot to vary the length. (Both are shown in Fig. 81. You can also use a drawing-pin and a piece of string but it is

Fig. 81   Commercial (above) and improvised beam compasses

hazardous.) Although one finds occasional dials where the original compasses went adrift, the centre must be accurately located. However, it is generally fair to assume that a dial was correctly written, and then one can establish the centre by marking the plug at the intersection of lines from 12.00 to 6.00 and 9.00 to 3.00, provided that the compasses confirm this location. If you are still doubtful, other methods can be found in an encyclopaedia or geometry textbook.

Fig. 82 Working board for painted dial restoration

There is no ideal sequence for inking – one is inevitably working above fresh ink somewhere, and the specialist may here in fact use some form of turntable with a raised beam to work from. A stable base for the dial is certainly essential and a rough wooden 'H' (Fig. 82) is satisfactory for taking care of the dial pillars. Start with the two broken rings which form the serifs (the heads and feet of the numerals), then proceed to the actual figures, and finally do the chapter circles round the minute divisions. The advantage of inking the serifs first is that they help to define the area of the numerals which has to be covered. If you go wrong or drop ink now, do not try to mop it up but leave it to dry and then scrape it off with a scalpel or Stanley knife. The partially inked Burgess dial is shown in Fig. 83.

While inking, it will be found with some dismay that the surface of the dial, though scrupulously cleaned, is not in fact at all consistent. In some parts ink will tend to run, while in others it will be difficult to make it stick at all, or it will produce a line of small globules. This is a situation which one has to make the best of – the professional restorer will probably repaint the whole surface. The additive in the ink helps and in bad cases use of a different pen or ink can ease the problem. The waviness of many surviving numerals suggests that the effect may be due to pollution of the backing paint over the years.

COLOUR-WORK

It is a pleasure now to turn from the tyranny of ruler and compasses. The coloured corners and centre-piece were left until last and in fact required

Fig. 83   Inking the Burgess dial

very little attention in this case. However, the gold swags needed restoring. There are many different 'gilding' preparations in the art-shop and the choice is not important, except that the wax products are unsuitable. Here Liberon 'Gilt Varnish' was applied with a brush.

Finally in the painting, there remained the actual chapter circles. Here three were evident, but often there is no sign of any, though it seems that a dial with no rings was rare and judgement has to be exercised as to whether to put them in. Inequalities of surface make inking them in with the compasses particularly difficult, but in practice they tend to be lost in the general effect anyway. The outer ring was often gold or red; there was no evidence here and it was penned in red.

FINISHING

Afterwards, there is an extended trimming and cleaning-up job with the scalpel – the dried ink chips off easily and the chance can be taken before lacquering to square up corners and edges, and to take out the odd splutter from the pen nib. Before committing to lacquer, hold the dial up to the light and wipe off any smears. The usual shellac clock lacquer is suitable and can be applied with cotton wool. Aerosol lacquers leave a distinctive 'modern' finish and can be very difficult to remove subsequently.

Dial-work is extremely concentrated and time-consuming – the charges of restorers are understandable, though considerable variation will be found and it is worth looking at restorers' samples. Judgement must be exercised as to whether a particular dial is to be assigned to a professional, but if damage is not too far-reaching much can be done by the amateur without harm for the future.

Fig. 84   Burgess dial restored

11   Setting Up and Testing

Both sides of the clock have now been overhauled and individually tested, and the ancillary parts have been considered. In this chapter we consider the remaining steps needed to get the clock going and to identify faults and difficulties which may still arise.

Oiling

Apply a drop of oil to all pivot holes and all mating surfaces, but *no oil* to the teeth of the wheels and pinions. Oiling is best done during assembly, before holes on the front plate are covered up, but it certainly must be done before the dial is fitted. It is thickening oil, to which dust and particles stick, which does much of the damage to the trains and, while oil is essential at the pivots, it can do nothing but harm to the train. The pallets are each given a drop of oil and so is any stud with a part moving on it (as, for example, the lifting piece, the Scott rack and rack hook). Date and lunar work, which are such a load on the clock, should be oiled similarly.

The seatboard is usually added at this stage, threading lines or chains with care (see below).

Test Stand

You can set the clock up for testing in its case, but access and visibility in the event of problems tend to be difficult. Several types of stand are used by clockmakers, but the simplest convenient compromise is probably a couple of angle-brackets screwed into the wall or shelf. There is no need for this to be at full running height (providing you do not cut the lines short yet). It is better to have the movement at a convenient height for observation and adjustment.

Fitting the Lines

When you have screwed on the seatboard, the thirty-hour chain or rope have to be hung so that the two greatwheels revolve anti-clockwise (see Fig. 38). The chain is most easily threaded with a length of stiff wire attached to the leading end. (For posted movements, see Part IV.) Start at the right and thread the chain over the striking pulley and ratchet and down through the seatboard hole. Leave a big loop and thread the weight pulley on to it. Now take the wire leader round to the left outside the plates and again thread it over the pulley and down through the seatboard. The counterweight is then threaded on and the last link closed or the rope joined (see Part IV).

The eight-day lines will already be fitted (see Chapter 6) and are now loaded with the pulleys and brought back up through the small seatboard holes. It is not critical, but generally these are best placed in the middle or at the opposite end of the barrel to that where the gut is fixed – often you will find old holes at back and front. The intention of the forward position is that the weight moves forward as it falls in the case, away from the pendulum when on a level with the bob. This is desirable because, in the confines of the case, bob and weight can interact and stop a clock mid-week in a mysterious fashion – a syndrome well known to repairers and not always easily cured. If, on the other hand, the weights tend to knock on the top edge of the plinth as the clock runs down, backward mounting of the lines may be a solution.

There are several ways of fixing the lines. The most traditional is probably winding the gut into a hank round your hand and making two half-hitches round it with the standing line. Another method is to make a small pile of knots, which can also be reinforced by a washer or ring of key-ring type. Again, one can tie the line tightly into a loop, with small pins of dowel or rod forming pegs across the holes. There is not a great deal to choose between these approaches. The essential is that the ends cannot possibly pull through the holes in the board. In this respect the pile of knots is least secure, and also looks untidy. Modern lines are often not supplied long enough to make a substantial hank, though this method has the advantage of being easy to undo if needed. Whichever method you use, leave determining the required length of gut, and cutting it, until you fit the movement into the case.

The correct length of line is reached when, completely unwound, the weights just clear the floor (with a small allowance for stretching). That they clear the ground is important, for if the lines are too long they can leave their barrels and, unwinding, coil round the barrel arbors themselves, leading to a seize-up. But the striking in particular must have a full run. If it runs out early and there is failure to strike, this may well stop the clock (symptom – the clock stops soon after 12.00 o'clock. Wind the striking and push the minute hand back a little, when the hour should be struck and free the movement). When fitting the line, ideally you need it under tension as you pass the end through the seat-board hole and secure it, which can be difficult (three hands needed). It is convenient then to have a small weight available (even a pair of pliers will do) to attach to the weight pulley, while the actual weight is placed alongside for gauging the height. The reason for all this care is the need to have the line winding regularly on the barrel grooves at the first winding (or laid regularly if, as with the Scott clock, the barrels are ungrooved). If it is correctly wound the first time, it will wind correctly on subsequent occasions. A clock where the gut has been wound on 'any old how' is likely to give chronic trouble.

Weights and Counter-weights

If the clock comes with a weight (or weights) it is often almost impossible to tell whether the weight belongs to it. A suitable range of weight is 6–8 lb (about 4 kg) for a thirty-hour clock, 8–10 lb (5 kg) for a four-wheeled train and 10–12 lb (6 kg) for an eight-day clock. A clock having date and lunar work may need up to 2 lb (1 kg) more. With eight-day clocks the heavier weight (if there is a difference) is given to the striking, on the left.

There is no reason to change the received weights unless, exceptionally, they are too light and you are absolutely sure that you have properly attended to the pivots and adjusted the escapement, and they still seem too light – for example because date and calendar work have now been restored to use. The best weight is certainly the lightest which will drive the clock, with a small surplus to take care of wear and congealing oil in the years ahead. Weights outside modern sizes (which vary somewhat within these ranges) are sometimes available from dealers. Pound-for-pound, lead is of course more compact, but cast iron is cheaper and was much used by the Victorians. According to taste, a coat of matt black paint may be given.

The pendulum's 'arc of vibration' is related fundamentally to the design and effectiveness of the escapement, but it is also influenced by the power applied. The swing should be sufficient to cause a clear recoil of the scapewheel teeth on the pallets, visible as a retreat of the seconds hand if there is one, and a 'supplementary arc' – swing after the tick – at the tip of the pendulum. In general, the pendulum will cover 6–7″ (150–180 mm) in all, of which some ½″ (1.25 cms) on each side would be supplementary arc, which is most easily assessed as the amount of recoil.

The counter-weight (of a thirty-hour clock) assists the chain or rope to stay on the greatwheel pulleys. It is normally a 'doughnut' ring of lead and readily available from suppliers. Both forms of line, rope and chain, can slip, especially if the best replacement chain is not a perfect fit or if you have not very well-closed open links in an old one. Slipping can be difficult to eliminate, but the situation is normally improved by fitting a heavier counter-weight of different form, for example wiring a small lump of lead to the existing weight ring. This may, of course, make necessary a slightly heavier driving weight. If this is not possible, or if the trouble (which is noisy, besides jeopardizing a run of full duration) persists, it may be necessary to consider fitting new pulleys with a chain made to fit. These are available as conversion kits from rope to chain drive and can usually be fitted without a lathe. Too thick or too thin a rope not only leads to short duration (because of slipping) but prematurely wears the rope.

Testing the Movement

GOING

With the striking locked, a wedge obstructing the fly, fit the pendulum and weight and test the going side. If necessary, re-adjust the height of the pallets as shown in Chapter 6. Once there is a satisfactory action with no teeth mislocking, consider the sound of the escapement – is it regular or is it limping?

Almost certainly it will sound irregular and the clock must then be 'set in beat' – adjusted to the level at which it is standing. This is done by slightly bending the crutch to one side or other, reaching round the movement and placing a finger of one hand near the top of the crutch to hold it, while with the other hand pressure is exerted lower down. You will have to experiment to see to which side the crutch should be bent. Slight, and not

Fig. 85   Marking of motion wheels setting

disfiguring, bends are all that are needed. Setting in beat may take some minutes – the final setting is very sensitive, being more a flexing than a bending of the crutch. The escapement is truly in beat when the ticks of the lockings are quite regular, sounding more like 'tock-tock' than 'tick-tock'. Once that is achieved, the going side should keep going and keep time, subject to regulation of the pendulum bob (see below).

The striking can now be tested under power, and no difficulty should be experienced if the trials in Chapters 7 and 8 were satisfactory, but now the two sides of the clock must be linked so that striking occurs exactly when the hand is on the hour. Fit the dial (temporarily) and place, but do not pin, the minute hand on its arbor. Bring it slowly round until the lifting piece drops off its pin and then relocate it (if necessary) free of the minute wheel so that it is pointing as nearly as possible to the hour. Often the correct positioning of the hand's square and the lifting pin was marked by the clockmaker by punching dots on the cannon pinion and on the minute wheel. In that case, theoretically, it has simply to be assured that the dotted tooth is assembled in the dotted space (Fig. 85). However, sometimes there is an abundance of dots (or scratches) left by previous repairers and it is safer to proceed as above. Where, with a three-wheeled train or single-handed clock the minute hand is driven by the greatwheel or there is no minute hand, adjustment can be made by slightly bending the lifting piece, making let-off earlier or later. In no case should it be necessary to bend a hand.

Stabilizing the Movement

Whether or not the movement is secured to the cheeks in the case seems always to have been a matter for individual decision. A screwed-down seatboard can be unnecessary and inconvenient to the repairer. However, brass-dialled movements, and those with painted dials and falseplates, are often dangerously unstable in their cases when weights and pendulum are removed, and it may well be worth fixing these seatboards. We favour drilling through the board into the cheeks and there sticking either plain metal (e.g. nail shanks) or dowel locating plugs, or short lengths of threaded brass. The holes are enlarged to be a loose fit for these insertions in the board (since a close fit makes them hard to locate) and, if threaded rod is used, washers and nuts (preferably wing-nuts) are added. Such a fixing not only holds the movement safely but also warns any subsequent repairer that it may be unstable. An unstable movement with sharp dial edges is of course a danger to itself and anyone inspecting it.

Fitting Hands and Dial

On the test stand you may not have the protection of a fixed seatboard, so assess the situation carefully and if possible apply the dial after fitting weights and pendulum.

It is almost possible to judge the quality of a movement from the fit of its hand and dial; the better the movement, the smaller the clearance in the central hole for the hour pipe, and the closer the hands (including the seconds hand) to each other. Consideration has always to be given to the need of hands to pass over each other without touching. Many a longcase clock stops perplexingly when all that is wrong is the lightest touching of the seconds hand on the dial or on the hour hand.

With a few exceptions, minute hands are secured by a pin through the arbor tip, and this has to be fitted with some care. The essential point is *first* to select a pin which fits the hole, later filing cut ends off flat. The domed collet (assortments available from suppliers) is then placed in front of the hand, pressed back against the bowspring's tension, and the long pin inserted. It is not satisfactory to have a situation where the tension on the hand is regulated by how far the pin is pushed in; the pin must fit and lodge in the hole even without the hand. Only when all is well is the pin cut so that it protrudes equally each side, and the ends filed flat. Dirty and mutilated pins and collets drastically spoil the appearance. Do not file a trench across the front of a collet to facilitate inserting the pin – this can stop the clock. Discard the original collet if it is in that condition.

There is an occasional problem with turning of the minute wheel as the dial is fitted (before the fitting of the hand prevents the cannon pinion from coming forward out of mesh under the pressure of the bowspring). This makes setting the hand to strike right on the hour very difficult. Solutions include raising the minute wheel on a washer, lowering the cannon pinion by flattening the bowspring, and temporarily wedging the minute wheel immediately after strike let-off, until the hand is fitted.

Regulation

Imagine yourself below the clock, looking up the pendulum. To speed it up, turn the regulating screw up, clock-wise. To slow it down, do the reverse, making sure that the bob drops with the nut. The amount required is best found by experiment but, with an average screw, one turn will produce variation of about one minute in twelve hours or nearly a quarter-of-an-hour in a week. One is, therefore, soon making only fractional movements of the screw. The effect of play in the motion-work varies. On single-handed clocks it can be very considerable, and there is something to be said for regulating against the sounding of the hour rather than against the dial. This should be consistent over twelve hours, despite the sizeable variation between hours which often occurs with the single-handed clock's starwheel. It is reasonable to expect a longcase clock, when regulated, to keep time to between one and two minutes a week.

Silencing the Striking

Many people declare that they cannot live with a striking longcase clock. This seems to be a fairly recent phenomenon, since very few of these clocks were provided originally with a silencing facility. It is not possible to modify them to 'daytime only' striking without unacceptable violation of the original clock, so what is to be done?

The immediate response is not to wind the striking, but with the thirty-hour clock you cannot, of course, do this, since one weight powers both going and striking. One solution is to wedge the fly in any way you fancy. The other is to inactivate the letting-off. You can do this by removing or pushing back the lifting pin so that it does not raise the lifting-piece. Alternatively, you can bend the brass lifting-piece of two-handed clocks, with the same effect. On a one-handed clock you can bend the long steel lifting-piece clear of the star-wheel which raises it. An ingenious compromise is to remove the countwheel (and possibly the bell) so that the clock strikes only 'one' at every hour. However, this might be as distracting as the complete strike.

With the eight-day clock it is possible to leave the striking unwound, but this is not advisable, since it is likely to stop the clock soon after 12.00 o'clock; despite the built-in precaution of a springy rack-tail and a bevelled edge to the snail, the rack tail can still stick on the snail when the rack falls, as it will continue to do; and this risk will remain if the course of wedging the fly is followed. It is necessary therefore to stop release of the rack. This is done either by bending the lifting-piece or pushing back (or removing) the pin in the lifting wheel with which it engages. Those few clocks which were made with a silencing device in fact normally use this method – the lifting-piece is mounted on a sprung arbor so that it can be moved by a hand lever in or out of the path of the lifting pin. Alternatively, a cranked lever is made to intercept a pin on the rack.

Faults and Diagnoses

This might seem a pessimistic note on which to end this section on movements, but in fact it is realistic. You may have cleaned and made good with scrupulous thoroughness and checked and tested throughout, yet, when all this is set up, the cherished movement will not perform as expected. This may surprise you, but it will not surprise the experienced restorer, to whom this is quite a common occurrence. To have everything correct does not necessarily mean that it will work together as a whole, day in, day out; too much interacts and too little is done (and has to be) by precise measurement for this to happen every time.

APPROACH

First, try to find the area in which the trouble is, initially whether in the going or striking. Even this may not be straightforward. For example, it may seem (it may even be) that the going is not getting sufficient power. Yet this does not necessarily indicate that there is trouble in the going train or the escapement (as there may be). It is possible that, on examination, the problem is found to occur shortly before each hour; in this case perhaps the effort of unlocking the striking is too much – either because there is not enough power, or because of other faults in the going, or because the warning piece is rough and unpolished, or the lifting-piece is tight on its stud – and so on. A fault on the striking side may indeed exist, but it may serve to show up inadequacies in the going. It may be that the time-honoured fault of not quite being able to drive the lunar or date disc is to blame – the reason why they were vandalized in the first place. Then perhaps the movement will run well without the dial – but possibly this is because the seconds hand was rubbing it. Perhaps changing the time of date and moon changes will help. Does their onset coincide with striking? Or perhaps the motion-work is tight, in which case the movement will run without the hands. Often the trouble is a coincidence of factors, each of which just passes muster on its own. While deduction can be applied, experimentation is often necessary, finding more than one fault for one symptom. And not always, it has to be admitted, knowing which enhancement actually wrought the cure.

THE GOING

One fault can almost be predicted in a newly set-up clock. Ironically, the better and more exact has been your work on the escapement, the more likely it is to occur. This is the jamming of the escapement when you hang the pendulum on the pallet cock. Particularly if the cock has no steady-pins, the weight of the pendulum is inclined to drag the pallet down minutely, reducing the drop on the entrance pallet and causing the escapement to seize up. Of course the remedy of slightly raising the pallets again is self-evident, but it can be a baffling fault if you are unprepared for it and have conscientiously arrived at a fine setting to your escapement.

The pallets of birdcage movements run in a cock planted on the top-plate and cannot be so easily moved up and down. Small adjustments can be made by filing the cock (to lower) or placing washers beneath it (to raise), but anything more radical has to be done by re-facing the pallet.

Unless there is something seriously wrong with the escapement, most troubles on the going side do in fact show themselves as lack of, or total absence of, power. This is detectable by how promptly a scapewheel tooth springs back against a pallet if pushed back and released, as was previously noted. Beware particularly if it seems to make a tiny spring forward and then land on the pallet rather gently – or not even get that far. This tends to indicate a hold-up in the train, and the commonest cause is a worn escape pinion, which filing may improve or which will have to be replaced or offset by moving the next wheel very slightly if possible. Similar wear in other pinions may also be the cause, as may malfunction of the gearing because a worn hole has not been drawn true. Another useful check is to ensure that the crutch is not binding on the pendulum – action of the escapement without the pendulum can be observed. The sides of the crutch should be polished and if necessary filed back, but they must be kept parallel, whether the crutch is of the closed or open-ended type. If you move the pendulum suspension block slightly forward or backward, the crutch should stay in place, not follow with it by friction. On the other hand, there must be no sideways 'click' from the crutch as the pendulum swings, because this amounts to lost impulse. The crutch must also be at right-angles to the plate.

If none of this helps, wedge up the striking and let the going train run a short distance without the pallets, assessing its freedom. If it was not before striking that the trouble occurred, but at less obviously regular times, when the clock stops use a felt-tipped pen or adhesive paper blobs to mark each wheel where it meshes with a pinion. Over an hour or two you can then see whether it is a particular engagement which regularly causes trouble. This often turns out to be a slightly bent wheel tooth or a worn pinion which now shows up because it has been reassembled in a new position.

Sometimes the escapement will be found to emit an elusive 'double tick', even though it may just keep going. This is likely to be due either to a loose crutch or to backs of some scapewheel teeth just snagging on the pallets. If left unattended it will lead to intermittent running.

THE STRIKING

It is worth restating here the golden rules for setting up either system, because the great majority of troubles with striking arise through their being neglected. They all apply to the situation when the train is locked and the striking is at rest. First, the hammer tail must not be resting on a hammer pin, and should ideally have just dropped off one. Secondly, the warning wheel pin must have a good run – about half a turn – before it is caught by the warning piece. (If, however, the run is excessive, there is the chance of the clock striking 'one' at warning.) Finally, the warning piece must be raised in place to catch the warning pin before the train is released.

In the thirty-hour clock the warning is usually controlled by a mechanical link between lifting and locking pieces. In the rack system it is controlled by the angle of the rack-hook's tail, which can be bent to adjust it. The setting of the hammer tail off the hammer pins is controlled ultimately by the position of the wheels between the plates (which have to be separated to make a change), although in the rack system there is some control by moving the gathering pallet to different positions on its square.

Again a common problem is 'lack of power', though this arises usually only in eight-day clocks. The load at striking consists mainly of the hammer spring and the rack spring on one hand, and the friction of the train and weight of the hammer on the other. You must be satisfied with the pivots and holes but, having seen to that, you may be able to reduce the tension of the springs without affecting their function. The function of the rack spring is to ensure that the rack will fall fully. This does not require a strong spring. (The choice of spring, which is of bent brass wire, probably does not arise; we are concerned with how far it is bent.) Ensure that the rack moves freely on its stud and then set the spring to the least tension that will send the rack tail to the bottom of the snail. There may be scope for similar adjustment to the hammer spring.

The other bugbears are 'continuous striking' and 'incorrect striking'. Continuous striking is caused by the gathering pallet's sliding forward or off its arbor, by the rack's behaving similarly, by loss of the rack pin on which the gathering pallet locks, or by breakage or loss of the rack stop-pin (driven into the frontplate) as a result of which the rack falls outside the gathering pallet's reach. The remedies here are obvious. Countwheel striking behaves in the opposite way if the countwheel is missed: it strikes single blows.

Incorrect striking is most unlikely to be caused by the 'program' – that is, the countwheel or snail. These parts do not wear or deform. The cause of trouble is likely to be in the warning or in mis-locking, whatever the system, and these have been considered in some detail in Chapters 6 and 7, as has the question of altering the rack. Where the principles have not been followed in setting up – for example, where the hammer tail rests on a hammer pin between strikings – incorrect striking, or failure of the train to get under way at all, are almost inevitable results.

Part III The Case

12   Tools and Materials

In general, tools for case repair and restoration are standard woodworking tools. Specialist tools, unlike those for movements, are in the main merely refinements of this norm. The few exceptions to this – for example, the veneering hammer – can often be made by the amateur, rather than being bought from a shop or tool supplier. The rules for buying tools are simple: buy the best you can afford, take care of the ones you have, buy as you need them and upgrade as you buy replacements. The list may appear rather formidable, but many can be obtained as the particular need arises and after you have assessed the situation as suggested in the next chapter. A selection of tools and materials is shown in Fig. 86.

1. Tools

— chisels. You need at least three – a one-inch (25 mm), a half-inch (13 mm) and a quarter-inch (6 mm) are suggested as a start. They must be kept very sharp. An old one-inch chisel is useful for removing old Scotch glue and in veneering, to save the blade of your good one.
— tenon or back saw. If you already have one of these, make sure it is really sharp. It may have served your grandfather well, but that almost inevitably means it will be blunt by now. At about £10 to £15 it is easier on the nerves and cheaper on the pocket to buy a new one rather than to invest in one of the several fiendish sharpening devices available. Buy a saw with hardened teeth – it will last you for years.
— screwdrivers. As in Chapter 3, making sure the tips are not chipped and twisted. Add one really big one with a metal shank right through the handle – the shank should come out of the other end and be peened over: This design means you will be able to use it for all sorts of things for which it was never intended!
— workbench. You are not likely to buy a workbench to overhaul one clock. If necessary, a Workmate and a trestle will suffice, or two trestles and a large sheet of thick ply. Even the kitchen table is not without use.
— vice. If you have a Workmate you might not need a separate vice, but if you can afford one buy a special vice for woodwork. You can use the type with a screw clamp if you are short of space, but suction-grip types are not recommended.

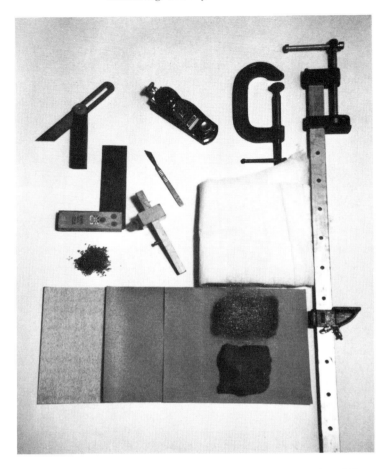

Fig. 86   Case-working tools. *Top to Bottom, left to right:* sliding
bevel, block plane, G cramp, sash cramp, try square, scalpel,
polishers' wadding, Scotch glue pearls, marking gauge, garnet
papers, coarse and fine steel wool

— straight edge or metal rule. Buy a good long metal rule, preferably 1 m;
then it can be used both as a straight edge and for measuring as well.
— clamps or cramps. It doesn't matter what you call them – you can never
have enough. Some are expensive, particularly the long sash cramps for
major case repairs, but they do not wear out and moreover they can be
hired from tool-hire shops for one-off jobs. Small G cramps are useful – a
couple of four-inch (100 mm) and a couple of eight-inch (200 mm), but buy
them as and when you need them, as quite often alternatives can be used.
— planes. For small repairs a block plane is very useful. These are about
five inches (125 mm) long, with adjustable mouths. For major casework a

jointing or smoothing plane is essential, but that sort of skilled work is really outside the scope of this book.

— hammers and mallets. A general-purpose mid-weight hammer is occasionally needed, but of more use is a large beechwood mallet. Mallets are not expensive.

— scalpels. You need these only for veneer and marquetry repairs, where the much abused Stanley knife is not really precise enough. Obtain them from a medical equipment supplier – a No. 3 handle and a couple of packets of No. 26 blades.

— gluepot. If you want to be really traditional and use Scotch glue for repairs (see Adhesives, below), you will need a gluepot. This is basically a double boiler and will seem quite expensive. You can in fact make do with a very large leakproof tin (i.e. catering baked bean size) and a smaller one (say rice pudding size) inside. Do not sneak off with the family saucepans or double boiler; once used for glue, they cannot be used again for cooking. Incidentally, empty food tins in general are ideal for storing and mixing liquids, and are cheap and disposable.

— brushes. A small selection of artists' (No. 2) sable brushes and half-inch (12 mm) decorating brushes will be needed.

— plastic resealable box. This is used constantly for keeping your polishing rubber damp if you use French polish.

— try-square. Check that it is accurate by placing against a square edge (such as a table edge). Draw a line, then turn the square over so it is facing the other way and redraw the line; if the two lines diverge at all, buy a new square.

— sliding bevel. This is basically a try-square where the metal arm is adjustable instead of being set at ninety degrees. It is used for copying angles from a piece of furniture to the wood which you are working on.

— marking gauge. A simple tool with a fixed point on one side and a sliding block with a thumbscrew-fitting to use as a fence. It is used for accurately transferring measurements from an original to the piece of wood you are working on. A ruler and calculation are less reliable.

2. *Materials*

Most materials will have to be bought from a specialist materials supplier (see p.229), because the necessary type and quality of polishes, stains etc. cannot be found at your local DIY store.

HARDWARE OR DIY STORE

— white spirit, methylated spirit, teak oil and genuine turpentine. You should be able to find all these without difficulty. Buy at least a litre of meths, the rest in the smallest quantities you can (250 ml or 500 ml).

— polishing cloth. An old cotton white shirt or handkerchief will do fine.

— stripper. Buy it if you need it (see Chapter 16). A general-purpose varnish and paint stripper is what you want. Anything that says 'peel off' or 'blanket style' stripper should be avoided – these can lift damaged veneers.
— paper towels. Buy a couple of rolls. They are cheap and disposable so, unlike rags, you will not be tempted to use the same one over and over again.
— old newspapers. Good for keeping other things clean.
— rubber gloves. *Essential* when using stripper, and useful at other times.
— wood. Small repairs can normally be done with scraps of the correct wood, but if you use the wrong variety no amount of colouring, polishing or staining will make it look right. Despite some authors' attempts to convince you otherwise, the days of breaking up old Georgian furniture are long gone. If you do not have a woodpile or heap of assorted scraps, you can buy broken pieces of 1930s solid oak furniture from junkshops very cheaply, but make sure it has no woodworm. Mahogany, pine, oak and other offcuts can often be had cheaply from a local joiners' firm or timber yard.

SPECIALIST SUPPLIERS

— abrasives. You will need a good selection. Garnet paper is better than sandpaper, because it clogs less and lasts longer. Buy a little more than you think you will need, particularly of the finest grades, because it can be stored indefinitely as long as it is kept dry. A selection of grits will be needed – say 80, 150, and 320. Buy a couple of sheets of 320 Silicon Carbide paper as well. This is grey in colour and contains a built-in lubricant which means that it is much better for fine rubbing-down of a polished surface. You will need a small quantity of steel wool in the finest grade possible; Liberon (see p.229) is best – no other supplier seems to get it quite as fine. Beware of the local hardware shop for steel wool – a lot of steel wool comes packed slightly oily to prevent rust and this will severely affect any refinishing you have to do. Coarse steel wool has its uses, but do not buy it until you have read the section on stripping (Chapter 16).
— adhesives. If you want to follow the traditional methods you will need Scotch glue and a gluepot. Kept dry, the pearl glue can be stored indefinitely. Special preparation is required before use (see Appendix). If using traditional glue does not appeal to you, use a PVA adhesive instead. This is the white woodworking glue that you can buy almost anywhere. Do not use the waterproof (exterior) variety; only the internal soluble glue can be loosened at some future date by your successors.
— polish. Buy only a Special Pale or Transparent (French) polish, in the smallest quantity you can, from a specialist supplier, when you need it. You will need only a small amount (say a litre) even if refinishing a whole case. All polish deteriorates over time and becomes useless without visible sign. Never buy inferior polish, and avoid anything which is muddy brown in

colour and opaque. The polish you want is a clear golden colour and will enhance the beauty of the wood rather than cover it.

— stains. Water-based stains are the best because they do not fade as quickly in sunlight and present few finishing problems, but they are generally available only from specialist suppliers. Naptha stains (the most common being the Colron range) are the next best, but they are incompatible with some finishing methods. Buy colours as you need them.

— sanding sealer. It is probably heretical for a restorer to include this, but it is one of the quickest and easiest ways of producing a reasonable finish, as well as being an excellent grain filler for difficult places. The same deterioration problem arises as with polish, so buy it in small quantities as you need it.

— earth pigments. These are cheap methods of suspending colours in a polish or wax, rather than dissolving them as in a stain. They are useful for concealing the edges of repairs, painting in grain and so on. They are opaque and cannot therefore be used to stain a piece of raw wood. Red ochre, yellow ochre, raw umber, brown umber, raw sienna, burnt sienna and vegetable black are among the colours you might use. If you can find a friendly restorer, he might sell you small quantities – the amounts required are tiny.

— waxes. The tinned versions are too soft and sticky. Make your own and have all your furniture (and clothes) smelling of beeswax! Get solid purified beeswax (not paste or liquid) and carnauba wax – a half-pound of each will last for ages. (See p.229)

— burnishing cream. This (from Liberon) is the restorer's secret weapon, the only all-purpose wood cleaning solution. It will remove heat and water rings in polish, years of grime and leave the polish silky smooth and shiny. It will also stain your clothes, smells terrible and is poisonous.

— polishers' wadding. Get the real thing if you can – cotton wool is unsuitable. Alternatively, try a small (say 2 ft square) piece of upholsterers' wadding, which is a little poorer in quality. It should be white, with a kind of skin on both sides and a flock, woolly substance in between. (The wadding is used for making your 'fad' inside the rubber used in French polishing.)

— wood bleach. Buy this only when you are sure that you will need it – it goes off in time, is poisonous and caustic and apt to be unpredictable in effect. Two-part bleach (A and B solutions) or oxalic acid crystals are the types to use.

— veneers. Again, buy them only when you definitely need them. Do not buy by post if you can avoid it, because careful matching is needed. Take a piece of the original veneer with you. There are many different types of mahogany, walnut and oak, and several different ways in which they can be cut.

Most finishing techniques, and quite a lot of repairs, are dirty jobs. Wear old clothes, or a long overall – then even if you spill nothing you will have something on which to wipe your hands!

13   Assessing the Case

Before you get to work on the case you need to decide how far you will go. Do you want your case to look brand new; or clean and free from defects; or really old and crusty, as if it had just been pulled out of a barn, but structurally sound?

There are some problems here, whatever your decision. If you go for authenticity, will you try to use old materials and methods throughout? If you take this path, who is to be deceived – the casual visitor who knows nothing about clocks, or the (possibly knowledgeable) person to whom you might eventually sell the piece? Is there perhaps an ethical problem here? If, on the other hand, you opt for the 'I can see it must be ever so old' reaction, how dilapidated will you permit it to be? Clearly these are matters of degree and compromise, but it is worth giving them some thought and trying to follow a consistent approach.

Inspection

Whatever you decide, you will need to examine the case for any repairs that need to be done before you can even think of touching the finish.

Consider first the structure (see Fig. 87), looking for any loose joints. You can do this by *lightly* twisting the case in various directions, looking for movement. Check inside whether any glue blocks are missing – they can be replaced at a later date, but if a whole line are missing this could indicate structural problems. (Fig. 88 shows structural defects on the Scott case.) Next, examine the side and front panels for splits that have been caused by shrinkage of the ground wood (below any veneer). Depending on where these occur, they can be considered major or merely cosmetic. However, the work involved in correcting them is quite tricky, so if you think a split is not too bad and not affecting the structure, you may decide to put up with it.

Inevitably, pieces will be missing from veneered, marquetry and cross-banded cases. They are not difficult to repair and colour well; seeing to them can produce a rapid improvement in the impression given by a case. Decide if you want any brass accoutrements (such as finials and

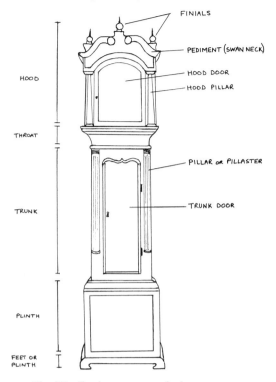

Fig. 87   Basic structure of a longcase

escutcheons) to look old and dirty, or whether they are to be restored clean and bright.

Then look at the finish. This is a subjective matter, but you will have to decide in due course whether the case needs stripping and repolishing, or just cleaning and waxing. It is not usually advisable to strip a case, but it may be necessary if, for instance, the finish has been botched and vandalized, the colouring wrecked by strident insertions of unsuitable wood or veneer. Stripping is a long and messy job and can create more problems than it solves. However, although many in the antiques trade hold the contrary view, our opinion is that it is sometimes necessary, and if the case is well finished afterwards it can enhance rather than lessen the value.

Here a word of warning: If you have a lacquered case, leave it alone. Extensive restoration is almost bound to have been carried out at least once already. These cases are valuable and the work required is extremely specialized, so leave it to a professional.

It is understandable that if you are confronting a good clock case you may be concerned lest your efforts make it worse and – horror of horrors –

Fig. 88   Structural problems in Scott case plinth

you have to go guiltily to a specialist after all. A certain caution is a good thing, but it can be overdone. There is much that the amateur with a little interest in woodwork can do for most neglected longcases. Everything suggested here is either reversible or, at worst, recoverable by a professional. However, do follow the golden rule of having some practice on scrap wood first.

The Burgess Case

Inspection of the Burgess case revealed no structural defects and no part of the case seemed loose. There was, however, a nasty split in the plinth front panel (Fig. 89) and examination showed this to be a major repair which

Fig. 89   Burgess plinth before restoration

would entail removal of the whole front of the plinth. This was such a considerable job mainly because the rosewood cross-banded circle had split as the panel had shrunk, and its true shape would need to be restored in the repair. The whole panel would have to be stripped and refinished. This would clearly be the main task with this case.

A look for more superficial defects showed that several pieces of cross-banding needed to be replaced and the brass finials cleaned. There were a few worm-holes (Fig. 90) in the base of the pilasters to be filled before considering the finish, which would entail thorough cleaning and a couple of coats of traditional wax polish.

The Scott Case

The Scott case was in a sorry state – absolutely riddled with woodworm, and with the back completely replaced by a sheet of hardboard, no doubt also because of worm damage. The tell-tale holes of the worm appeared all over the surface and, since invariably there is more damage beneath the surface, some tricky decisions had to be taken. If you are thinking of buying a longcase clock for restoration, avoid one like this! The hardboard back and the sheer number of holes on the surface, together with the estimated hidden damage, meant that the best course of restoration would

Fig. 90   Worm-eaten pilasters on the Burgess clock

be simply to try to stabilize the structure rather than completely rebuild the case. Closer inspection yielded signs that the original footings were missing and had been in the form of a plinth rather than feet. This would have to be replaced (Fig. 91).

There was a small split in the main plinth (Fig. 88), with some lines of stringing missing from the trunk (stringing is inlaid lines, usually of boxwood and black ebonized wood, for decoration). Also the cheeks – that is, the two pieces of wood which support the seatboard in the case – were structurally unsound owing to worm damage and would need replacement (Fig. 92).

On the hood, the glass was broken on the door and would need replacement. A piece of veneer had been crudely nailed into place on the door. The pediment needed a small repair and there were signs of three missing finials, one between the swan-necks and one at each front corner.

The hood capitals were gilded and required cleaning, as did the two typical rosettes on the swan-necks. The overall finish of the case was not perished or destroyed, but it was filthy and would need a lot of cleaning.

Fig. 91   Plinth of Scott case

Fig. 92   Worm-eaten cheeks to Scott trunk

and of course the worm-holes needed to be disguised. The new plinth and other repairs would have to be suitably stained and 'distressed' so as to blend with the rest of the case. The finish would probably be a couple of coats of traditional beeswax polish.

14 Structure and Repairs

Basic Longcase Construction

Longcases come in a huge variety of proportions, structures, materials and finishes – it could not be otherwise over a period of nearly 200 years. Here we shall be focusing on our two example clocks. They are common early Victorian types, but many of the points made will apply equally to older clocks.

The basic structure is shown in Fig. 87. It is made up of three

Fig. 93 Original glue-blocks

components: the hood, the trunk and the plinth. The hood is a completely separate structure (although the back runs up behind it in one piece), and we will deal with this on its own later. The trunk and plinth are simple boxes joined together with a common back.

The backboard, round which the case is built, usually consists of two or more planks of wood (pine or sometimes oak) glued and cramped together, and it is quite common for these to separate with age. Access for the owner is always from the front; where access to the clock movement is from the sides or back, the case is almost certain to be a modern reproduction. The sides of the case are butt-jointed to the common back of plinth and trunk and, particularly in the nineteenth century, small square or triangular blocks of wood were glued inside the case to reinforce these joints (Fig. 93). The butt joints were sometimes strengthened with nails, and sometimes also rebates (grooves) were made in the sides to house the backboard.

Oak and pine cases generally have their sides and fronts made up of solid timber, sometimes veneered or cross-banded in the front for added decoration. Mahogany and walnut cases, on the other hand, are generally not solid; the carcase is made of pine (sometimes referred to as 'deal') or oak, with mahogany or walnut veneer laid over the top of the panels and disguising the joints. There are two main reasons for this. Mahogany and walnut were expensive hardwoods, so the use of oak or pine as a carcase saved money. Secondly, figured woods, such as flame mahogany and burr walnut, have a greater tendency to shrink, warp and crack. Of our examples, the Burgess clock is (quite typically for a thirty-hour clock) of oak, but with fairly elaborate decoration, while the Scott clock is similarly oak but (again typically of an eight-day clock) far more extensively covered with mahogany.

Fig. 94   Structure of top trunk moulding

The mouldings found at the joint of plinth and trunk, at the top of the trunk and on the hood itself, are very important in the visual effect of the clock and also reflect date (as outlined by several of the books in Further Reading). They were made of the same material as the visible parts of the case but, like the main case, were often not solid. To save on hardwood, they would be built up on a triangular core of pine or oak, as can be seen from behind the case (Fig. 94).

The hood is less complex in construction than it looks at first glance. On the earliest clocks it could be raised upwards and caught on a catch, but in the great majority of longcases the hood slides forward on runners. If the hood does not have a hinged door (a situation quite common on thirty-hour clocks), the hood had to be moved forward for setting the hands and, as a result, the runners can be badly worn. However, a hinged door is commoner and this may be flanked by pilasters which are either part of the door or mounted separately from it (depending partly on date and locality). The hood was a simple box structure, jointed like the rest of the case, to which might be attached smaller boxes and blocks, with or without mouldings, carvings or decorative fretwork.

The corners of hood doors are variously mitred at 45° or made at right-angles, but the structure under the veneer is always square (with the top and bottom between the two sides). On whether or not to mitre the veneer, practice seems to have varied.

Decoration

Cases of all periods vary enormously in the amount of decoration used, from the plain oak case (of any date) to the ornate lacquered cases, mainly of the early eighteenth century. Forms of decoration used include:

inlay – lines and small shapes of contrasting wood set into the main body.

veneer pictures – floral or similar (marquetry) and geometric (parquetry) designs cut in contrasting veneers and then laid on as a sheet, often elaborately symmetrical.

cross-banding – a thin wood or veneer, usually following the lines of the case, but with the grain direction running at 90° to that of the main part of the case.

pilasters – columns set into the two front corners of the hood and, later, those of the trunk. These might be plain or reeded for their whole or part-length and their style and length can help in establishing a date and locality for the clock.

capitals – tops and feet of pilasters. They may be of lacquered brass or gilt-wood.

finials – of lacquered brass or wood, often gilded. These finials, spikes, eagles and others designs were placed symmetrically on top of the hood and, if missing, are often evidenced by holes or mini-plinths.

frets – usually in the earlier days an ornamental fret might be placed on top of a flat hood as a crest. On the better clocks, wooden (occasionally brass) frets were set below the top moulding of the hood and lined with silk, being partly ornamental and partly functional to let the sound out without letting the dust in. Thirty-hour clocks not uncommonly have a plain hole in the top of the hood for this purpose. Side windows in the hood are again some help in dating and may be fretted, but it is not always easy to tell whether these openings were at one time glazed – nor how far giving sight of the movement inside was their purpose.

Major Case Repairs

Major case repairs may well include attention to one or more of the following: warping, loose backboards, splits and general looseness. Of these, some can be rectified by the amateur, some are best left to the professional restorer, and in others this decision will depend on the severity of the damage.

WARPING

This may be part or all of the case and involves some form of twisting or cupping of the timber. We strongly recommend that serious instances are left to the professional restorer. There are several 'home-made' remedies often suggested, including weighing the offending board down on damp grass, or cramping the warp straight. Unfortunately these do not address the fundamental cause of the trouble, that of some inherent stress in the wood due to its drying out over the years. What tends to happen after these improvised treatments is that the warp gradually returns. A professional restorer will relieve the stresses by making saw-cuts in the back of the board, or by filling the cuts with wedges in the case of a warp that goes the other way, or perhaps by counter-veneering the reverse side of the warp to try to pull it back into shape.

Warping of trunk doors is extremely common, because they are basically unattached and the grain runs lengthwise. The curious state of the Scott clock's trunk door is a good example. As will be seen from Fig. 95, it has been reduced in thickness to the point where it could be strained flat, and then supported by a structure of braces (Fig. 96). One frequently comes across trunk doors which have (presumably) been strained flat without reduction, by a couple of stout oak battens and large-headed screws behind. Warping may also be the explanation of the large number of cases which clearly have replaced trunk doors – it is, after all, hardly likely that a

Figs. 95 & 96   Strengthening battens on thinned Scott door

door would be lost. The Scott solution is very drastic and, in our opinion, not very elegant.

LOOSE OR CRACKED BACKBOARDS

While they are a major part of the structure, longcase backboards do not (as do backs in some other clocks), take the direct weight of the suspended pendulum, which of course hangs from the movement. Provided the rest of the case is not loose as well, they are not difficult to rectify. If the joint between two pine boards has gone, they can be removed from the case. After letting in a little hot water in the join of the side and back to soften the glue, lever them off gently. Clean where the two boards meet, planing if necessary to ensure a good close fit and making sure that any old glue has been removed (with a chisel, and hot water if necessary). Lay the boards next to each other and glue along the joint. Rub them together once or twice and cramp them up in sash cramps. These should be laid alternately about six inches to a foot apart, one above and one below the boards, to ensure that excess glue is squeezed out (see Fig. 97). (Perhaps at this point

Fig. 97 Arrangement of cramps for
holding panels

we should remind you that, though sash cramps like these are a considerable investment, they can be hired for a special job.)

In doing this, remember that the key to a good joint is not how much glue you put in, but how much you can get out! Cramps of any sort should not need to be screwed up really tightly, but just enough to hold the joint firm while it is drying – if you need to force the joint closed with the cramps then you have probably not cleaned it up well enough in the first place. Once you have clamped the joint, leave it overnight to set; do not be tempted to loosen the cramps 'just to check how it's going'.

Once the joint is set, the completed board can be replaced in the case. This entails laying the back in its grooved rebates (if any) and pinning it with panel pins set about a foot apart. These pins will obviate the need for clamping and, although it is not normally acceptable to use nails in restoration, they would have been used here originally.

SPLIT PANELS

There are two techniques available to deal with split panels. One is to insert a thin sliver of the appropriate wood in the split, clamping and glueing it in. When it has dried, a plane, and then garnet paper, are used to make the insertion smooth with the surrounding surface. In due course this has to be coloured and re-finished (Fig. 98).

The second method, which was used here (on the Burgess case), is to remove the actual panel in its entirety, glueing the split closed (Fig. 99). Then more wood has to be added (inside the cross-banding) to make up the missing width (Fig. 100). After carrying out this repair, the panel was glued back and held by a few panel pins (as above), in the knowledge that

Fig. 98   Filling a split plinth panel

the cross-banding round the edge of the panel would be replaced and that this would conceal the pins in exactly the same way that the original joints were covered. Sash cramps were used to hold the panel in place while drying. The completed repair is shown in Fig. 101.

GENERAL LOOSENESS, DISMANTLING AND RE-ASSEMBLY

If (after examination as described in Chapter 13) the case feels structurally unsound, each section will have to be reglued after dismantling and cleaning, and the glue blocks replaced.

To dismantle the case, first remove any glue blocks. This is done by placing a wide chisel flat at the joint of block and case, and giving it a hard tap with a mallet, when it should come away easily. If after a couple of attempts there is no success, check that some bodger has not nailed the block surreptitiously to save him glueing it on when he repaired it. If you can find no nail, the glue must be softened (as must be done for all the joints) by injecting hot water with a hypodermic.

After dismantling the relevant sections, thoroughly clean off old glue and reglue them. Do not attempt to square up joints so that they are at 90°, as a cabinet-maker would now if he were making a new case. Not all longcases were square when they were made – some were built by village carpenters and coffin-makers, while others were made by craftsmen of the

Fig. 99   The split closed up

Fig. 100   Making up the width of the closed plinth panel

Fig. 101   Repaired Burgess plinth

highest skill and experience. Glue the joint as you find it. Any attempt at correction could lead to enormous amounts of unnecessary work.

Glue blocks are fitted differently according to the type of glue employed. If you use the traditional Scotch glue, it can be brushed on and then the block pushed into place, rubbing it up and down slightly two or three times to exclude air and excess glue. Using PVA (white) glue means that each block will have to be glued and held in place for a short time while the glue dries, since white glue does not have the same instant 'tack' as Scotch glue. If using this method you will need to hold the blocks in place while they dry, but ensure that the pins are removed afterwards. The glued joints should all be clamped up overnight, regardless of which type of glue you are using.

WOODWORM

It is extremely common for a longcase to have woodworm damage, since the timbers are undisturbed for long periods. Damage can be superficial, as in the Burgess case where it is confined to the capitals of the corner pillars (see Fig. 89) or extensive (as in the Scott clock, Fig. 102). The worms prefer the soft backboards, so be particularly careful to check the back for the tell-tale holes. These holes are the result of small grubs that have hatched out of their eggs, laid in corners and cracks, and which burrow through the wood until breaking through the surface to become flies – laying eggs and starting the cycle all over again.

If you do find any holes, always investigate. The damage may not be recent but can extend far under the surface and cause major structural defects. In fact it is normally hardly worth establishing if the worm is dead

Fig. 102   Severe woodworm infestation

or alive – if you see holes, treat them before doing any other jobs.

The first course of action is to treat the worm with a poisonous fluid to kill off any remaining and prevent their spreading to other bits of furniture. The insecticide can be bought from your local DIY store and comes either in a small can with a built-in injector, or in a larger one for brushing on. Follow the instructions, being sure to wear gloves. Start with the interior of the case, getting right into any nooks and crannies, and move on to do the outside back. Polished surfaces can be treated – the fluid will not penetrate the polish but it will drop into the holes, killing any live grub there. Avoid getting the fluid on any bare pieces of wood that will require finishing later (for instance anywhere where the finish has worn through) as the fluid can cause staining problems.

It is almost impossible to list the repairs that may be necessary to a woodwormed case. If, as was the case with the Burgess clock, you have a small amount of damage that does not affect the structure, then the holes can be filled after treatment. Use a piece of matchstick glued in each hole and then a skim of two-part filler over the top. Anything more severe than this (check, using a brad-awl, or by lifting a small piece of veneer to see if the ground has been eaten away) is likely to require complex and extensive repairs, sometimes necessitating lifting all the veneers, cutting back to good wood, and then rebuilding – not usually a job for the amateur. You may just decide that the expense of reconstruction is not worth it and you can put up with the appearance, provided the structure is not affected.

Base Repairs – The Scott Case

The Scott case was a prime example of extensive worm damage. Simply to

Fig. 103   Previous repair to Scott plinth

Fig. 104   Insertion of new wood in   Fig. 105   Structural repair to plinth
               Scott plinth

make and fit a replacement plinth involved removing a section of the base and replacing it. The tell-tale sign was not just the presence of worm holes all over the case, but the obviously poor attempt at filling a corner of the base (Fig. 103). This could have been attributed to someone's attempting a quick botch of a repair, but it was clear by looking from underneath that there was in fact no sound wood with which a better job could have been done.

The veneer had to be removed (as with the cross-banding on the Burgess case) and the ground wood cut back and replaced. The worm damage was so severe that it was necessary to fit a length of pine batten to give some support to the repaired section, but fortunately this will be hidden when the clock is standing in its normal position (Fig. 104). Fig. 105 shows the completed repair, with pine bracing, from the back.

It was obvious that there was something missing from the base of this case (Fig. 103). Below the bottom run of mahogany cross-banding was a blank piece of ground wood. Markings indicated that the same thing was missing from the sides, and we were able to conclude that in fact there was a subsidiary plinth missing. This is quite a common fault on antique longcases, caused by the relative fragility and susceptibility of this area to damage from knocking, worm and even rot from damp floors.

A little research in reference books gave a good idea of what form the replacement should take. Photographs of similar cases showed that there had been a shallow oak plinth with a moulding along the top edge.

The procedure for such a restoration is as follows. Cut the lengths of wood required, making sure that they are a little oversize, allowing for a

Fig. 106   Using a moulding plane

Fig. 107   Mitreing the new plinth moulding

run-off while making the moulding and for the mitre at the front corners. Decide what sort of moulding is appropriate and plot it out on the pieces of wood. Moulding can be made up in various ways – by hand with chisels and abrasive, by moulding planes or with a router. Using a router is probably the easiest, but the cutters are costly and the range restricts your choice of shapes. Making up mouldings by hand with chisels, abrasives and rasps is extremely hard work and rarely consistent over a long stretch. It can be eased by making cutters from old chisel and plane blades (or similar), sharpening them and using them as shaped scrapers.

    In some ways the best solution is moulding planes, which can often be bought for £2 or £3 each at car boot sales and are an excellent investment

Fig. 108   Glueing the new sub-plinth   Fig. 109   The new structural work in
the plinth

for the restorer. They are obviously harder work than with a router, but
they enable you to get a wider range of shapes at much less cost. They are
used at an angle (unlike a normal plane – see Fig. 106) and you can either
use just one of the required profile or use a combination to achieve the
moulding which you want.

Of course, if this sounds like too much work or expense, you can
probably get a local cabinet-maker to run up something on his spindle
moulder. This will cost a little more in terms of labour, but will save you
spending out on tools if you do not already have them. While it is possible
to buy ready-made mouldings, these are usually for kitchen units etc. and
are not in the woods or shapes that you will need. When you have made the
mouldings, you can do the mitres. It is a good idea to use a mitre box for
accurate results (Fig. 107), but double-check your measurements and draw
the mitres on before cutting; if you make a mistake here – cutting the mitre
the wrong way round – you will have to go back to making moulding all
over again.

Glue the new sub-plinth in place and cramp it up overnight, in several
stages if necessary, adding glue blocks for extra support (Fig. 108). Fit a
square block in each corner (see Fig. 109), making it just a fraction longer
than necessary; this will support the weak mitre joints, protecting the front
of your new plinth if the case is moved, and helping to transfer some of the
weight of case and movement from the 'skirt' to the main load-bearing
structure of the case. The new plinth is then stained and finished.

15   Veneer Repairs

The most common form of ordinary wear and tear is missing and damaged pieces of veneer. Our thirty-hour case is no exception to this, and has suffered missing cross-banding in several places – not to mention that which we had to remove in order to repair the split plinth front.

Veneers – Thickness and Cutting

Older veneers were much thicker than today's machine-produced varieties, but this does not necessarily present much of a problem. While it is possible to cut veneers from solid wood, this is normally done only if the right sort of wood is available as veneer or for extremely high quality pieces of furniture where keeping to original methods and materials is of paramount importance (museum work, for instance – Fig. 110). The simple way of making a thicker veneer is to stick two layers of thin veneer together, glue and cramp them in place (using wood blocks to spread the load and prevent marking) and leave them overnight to dry.

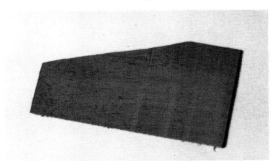

Fig. 110   Special thick veneer

Veneers are much easier to cut when damp, being less inclined to split. Wet both sides with a damp cloth and place between two boards overnight to flatten them before cutting. Use a scalpel if you have one – the blades are much finer than a Stanley knife, and that helps avoid splitting. However, it is important to remember not to glue wet veneer (unless with Scotch glue), because the damp may affect the adhesive properties. Once it is cut, therefore, put your veneer back between the boards to keep it flat while it dries for use.

Removing Veneers

Old damaged veneers can be removed quite easily with a little patience. You need an electric hot-air gun of the type used in stripping paint, also a pot of hot water and an old chisel or decorators' large spatula. Find a piece of veneer that is already lifting, or that has an edge showing, and use that as a starting-point. Work the hot-air gun over this area, keeping it six to eight inches above the surface, while at the same time trying to ease the wet chisel or spatula gently under the veneer. As soon as it starts to lift, move the gun on a bit further and push the chisel further in. Keep removing the chisel and re-dipping it in the hot water. You should be able to lift up the veneer in one piece this way, so that if required it can be reused. The trick is not to try too hard – let the hot-air gun and the hot water do the work in softening the original Scotch glue, rather than trying to prize up the veneer (see Fig. 111.)

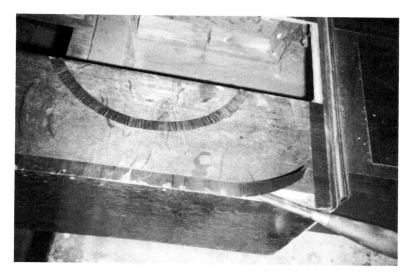

Fig.111 Raising trunk edge veneer

This method of removing veneers will, unless you are particularly expert, ruin the finish, so it is normally better to strip the area first (see Chapter 16 – 'To Strip or Not to Strip'). If you are planning to re-use the same veneer – perhaps because, as with the Burgess clock here, you had to remove it merely to gain access for another task – then as soon as you have lifted the veneer off the carcase, wash all the remaining glue from the back with hot water and a stiff brush and place the cleaned piece between boards to keep it flat while it dries.

Fitting Veneer Patches

Restoration does not usually involve large areas of re-veneering. Instead, you will probably find that there are several small pieces of veneer missing. These are far less of a problem to replace than they first seem, and they can be fitted using either Scotch or white glue, though the approaches differ somewhat.

OCCASIONAL PATCHES

First of all, you will need to select an appropriate patch of replacement veneer. This should be of the correct wood and with as close a match in grain and figure pattern as possible. The match in colour is not nearly as important because it can be altered later.

Fig. 112   Patching veneer

Never try to cut the veneer exactly to the shape of the hole at this stage (unless it is marquetry, in which case see below). This invariably results in a bad fit. It should be oversized, and the appropriate shape will vary according to the context of where the patch is to be inserted. On missing pieces of cross-banding you can cut it square, but on other pieces you will need to cut at least one side, and possibly all sides, in a more irregular shape (see Figs. 112, 113). This is not so much for ease of fitting – indeed,

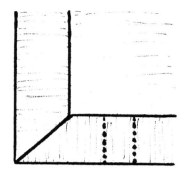

Crossbanding

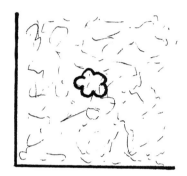

Patch in burr veneer. Very irregular in shape, as straight lines are difficult to disguise in burr woods. Special punches can be bought to make identical holes in wood and patches to fit

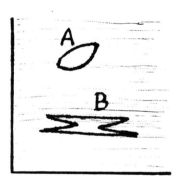

Centre of panel
A Traditional boat shape patch
B More tricky, but easier to blend 'zig-zag' patch

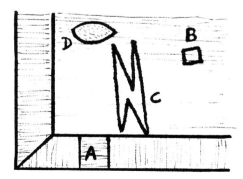

Badly fitted patches
A Patch goes the wrong way
B Too regular in shape – stands out
C Long lines cutting directly across the grain – very difficult to disguise
D Grain distribution clearly different to surrounding wood

Fig. 114   Placing the veneer

Fig. 115   Angled cutting of veneer patches

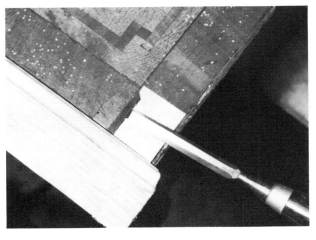

Fig. 116   Trimming the patch

it makes the fitting slightly more complex – but because it will save you time when trying to blend the patch in so that it is almost invisible. The main thing to avoid is any lines that will cut across the grain of the surrounding wood at ninety degrees.

The next step is to lay the veneer over the hole (Fig. 114), making sure that you have oriented the grain in the right direction. Look at it carefully to check that it is right, because there will soon be no going back! Then carefully hold down the patch while cutting round its outline with a scalpel. Angle the blade inwards while cutting, to ensure a really tight fit (Fig. 115). If you do not cut right through the old veneer in one go it does not matter, so long as you have clearly marked the outline for cutting afterwards.

When the patch is cut to size, use a small chisel to remove the waste (Fig. 116) – if it does not pop out you can use a little hot water to dissolve the glue – and then try the patch in the hole. If it is not a perfect fit, then a slight trim is probably all that is necessary. Note that it is better to trim the hole than the patch at this point because the patch will be very weak in places until glued to the groundwork.

For glueing, you can use Scotch glue – which obviates the need for clamps, and so is particularly useful in the centre of panels or small awkward corners – or the white PVA glue. If using white glue, spread it

Fig. 117   Glueing a veneer patch

thinly on the hole and patch, and have your clamps ready with cork or wooden blocks to prevent marking (Fig. 117).

There are two things to be very careful of when using white glue to repair veneers, particularly thin modern veneers. One is to use the glue sparingly, and the second is that you must not cramp up too tightly. If you neglect either of these points the glue can squeeze through the pores of the bare veneer to the surface, which will make finishing very difficult. These problems do not occur with Scotch glue because it is completely water-soluble and so residues can be washed away.

MARQUETRY

For marquetry a slightly different technique is appropriate. In this case use tracing paper to trace carefully round the outline of the missing piece. Stick the tracing to your veneer patch with a very thin coating of Scotch glue and leave to dry under a board to keep it flat. You will need a fret – or piercing – saw, and also a home-made marquetry sawing table (which can be a piece of wood with a vee cut in it and can be mounted in a vice – see Fig. 118). The saw is used vertically and gently moved up and down in the centre of the vee, following the tracing with the patch stuck to it. (The points of the blade teeth should point downwards to the handle, cutting on the downward stroke.) It is best to have a scrap piece of veneer under the patch while cutting; otherwise you will tend to tear out the back of the veneer with the cutting edge of the saw. Afterwards the veneer and tracing can be separated with a little hot water.

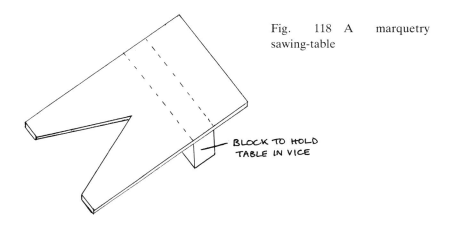

Fig. 118 A marquetry sawing-table

BLOCK TO HOLD TABLE IN VICE

Fig. 119   Home-made veneer hammer

Veneering with Scotch Glue

GENERAL PROCEDURE

Traditionally, all veneering was carried out with Scotch glue. While this is more complex than with modern glues, it has several advantages – not least that you can have as many goes as you need to get it right. For this method you will need Scotch glue (prepared as in the Appendix), an old chisel (preferably fairly blunt), some brown paper, sticky parcel tape, an old iron and a veneer hammer.

You can buy a fancy veneer hammer from a specialist supplier, but it is much cheaper to make your own out of hardwood (see Fig. 119). The main part is a block of beech, shaped to a rounded point at one end, and the handle is a piece of dowel. Drive the handle into place rather than glueing it; the handle will spend a lot of time in hot water and this would simply soften the glue – you do not actually use the handle while veneering, except for transporting the hammer from your hot water pot.

'Hammer veneering', as this method is called, is really a misnomer, as the hammer is used not to beat the veneer into place but more like a squeegee to squeeze out excess glue. The chisel and hammer should be kept in hot water all the time they are not being used in this operation – you can use the ready supply of hot water left over from heating your glue. As the iron needs to be kept fairly hot over a period of time, it is best to use an electric iron – but do not use a household iron or you will ruin it for domestic use. Practice will soon tell you the degree of heat needed. A

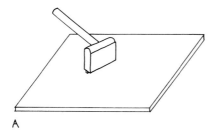

Fig. 120   Hammer veneering

A   Shows hammer at start of stroke

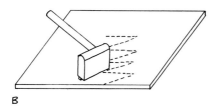

B   Shows path of hammer stroke, squeezing excess glue out to the edge

general guide is that spittle will hiss on the iron plate when a working temperature is reached. Finally among the preparations, your veneer should be slightly damp throughout the whole procedure.

First spread some glue over the area to be veneered, quickly lay the veneer on top and press it down. The natural 'tack' of the glue should hold it, but do not worry if some bits have not stuck down because the glue has cooled, so long as there is some glue there to do the job when the time comes. Place the iron on a small area to warm the glue (if the iron is at the right temperature it will hiss on the damp veneer). After a second or two lift it and drag the hammer in a zig-zag movement from the centre outwards; the iron will remelt the glue and the hammer will squeeze all the excess glue out from underneath while pressing the veneer down firmly (see Fig. 120).

When you are happy that the veneer is flat and positioned where it should be, with the hot wet chisel clean up the excess glue that you have squeezed out. If at first you cannot get the veneer flat or the glue cools and you are unable to press it out, just use the iron again for a few seconds to remelt it. This can be done as many times as required.

JOINING VENEERS

To join two new pieces of veneer, either side-to-side or end-to-end (as in the cross-banding on the Burgess case), you stick the second piece as just described, but allow it to overlap the first by about 3 mm. Iron it and hammer it as before, then carefully cut through the double thickness of veneer at the centre of the overlap. With your hot wet chisel gently lift up the second piece of veneer at the overlap and pull out the sliver of veneer underneath to throw away. Use the hammer and iron as necessary to smooth back the veneer and make a perfect joint (Fig. 121).

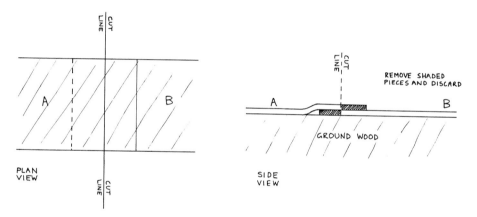

Fig. 121   Butt jointing veneers

To butt join piece A to B, (as in crossbanding for instance), glue both down so that A overlaps B. Cut through both pieces at the same time along the line shown. Then, using a hot, wet chisel, remove the top excess piece and discard it, lift the overlap slightly and remove the bottom excess. Use the veneer hammer or clamp to make a perfect butt joint

When you have completed as much as you are going to do in that session, moisten pieces of sticky paper tape and place them over all the joins that you have just made. Wet the reverse (upward) side once in place so that the tape becomes almost transparent. Leave the veneer to dry out as long as possible – at least a few days and preferably, if you have the patience, up to a month, to allow the job to settle down. The veneer will shrink slightly as it dries. The purpose of the brown tape is to counter the shrinkage of the veneer drying; as the tape dries, it pulls the join together tightly.

Once you have decided that the join is dry enough, you can clean up, ready for refinishing. Remove the brown tape by dampening it and scraping it off gently with your blunt chisel. Sand off any excess glue that has dried on, and also any places where the veneer overhangs the edge fractionally because you did not cut it right in the first place. Use garnet paper downwards over the offending edge – if you use it upwards you could peel off a large piece of veneer. If you are not happy with your finished result, you can always start again by heating up the glued veneer with the iron or hot-air gun, and then re-lay it as before.

The above method can be used only on flat surfaces. If you need to veneer curved surfaces on a clock case – most mouldings are made from (thin) solid wood which may be glued round a pine frame – then you will need to use heated sandbags instead of the iron and the hammer to hold the veneer in place while the glue melts and then gradually cools and dries.

Repairing Stringing

As already explained, stringing comprises inlaid narrow lines, normally of boxwood (light in colour) or of black stained wood (simulating ebony). The lines are used to provide a contrasting detail to the edge or corner of the case, or to define a panel. On cases that are veneered, particularly with cross-banding right to the edge, the stringing adds an extra little bit of quality, and protects the fragile end-grain edge of the veneer from being snagged on clothing or while cleaning.

The Scott case had a small section of stringing missing – a simple sandwich of boxwood, 'ebony', and then boxwood again. This needed to be replaced, then coloured and polished to blend it with the original. You can buy ready-made stringing from the veneer merchants in a good variety of sizes, but for more complex patterns you will probably have to make up your own for a close match. The three pieces of stringing (Fig. 122) were glued together in sandwich form before fitting, taking care to make the section over-long to allow for cutting to size. This is especially important in cases which have had bad worm, as often a piece that looks all right when untouched will crumble when you attempt to cut it. After cramping up overnight – for small flat pieces like this it is easier to leave them in the vice than to use G-cramps – the replacement piece is ready for fitting.

Clean out the slot or groove of any old glue or pieces of old stringing, and make sure that there is a firm base for the stringing to adhere to (again,

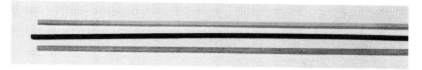

Fig. 122   Sandwiched stringing

especially on worm-ridden cases). If you are fitting the replacement in the middle of a line, cut its ends so that they are at an oblique angle. This makes them easier to disguise at the finishing stage. If, as on the Scott case, you are fitting a piece that will have to butt into a joint or corner, cut the replacement to the relevant angle (usually, but not always, a mitre of 45°) at one end only. All cutting of stringing lines, unless very wide or thick, should be done using a chisel as a guillotine onto a scrap piece of wood. It is much easier to be accurate with a sharp chisel than with a saw on such small pieces.

Next, lay the replacement piece in the position it will occupy, and use a sharp knife or scalpel to mark the angles of the ends on to the wood below. Remove your replacement piece, cut along the marks and clear the waste. Your repair piece should drop straight in for a perfect fit (Fig. 123). It is very important that you cut the replacement piece first, rather than cutting the original – if you do it the other way round you will spend hours trying to get the angles to match exactly, with your replacement piece getting smaller and smaller until you either give up or have to start all over again.

Fig. 123   Fitting the stringing (case on its back)

More complex stringing can be made up using the sandwich technique to obtain the patterns required (see Fig. 124).

FIG. 124   MAKING UP INLAYS

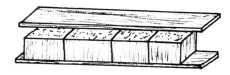

(a)   Chequered line inlay   (b)   Making your own crossbanding

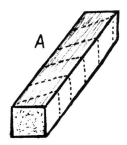

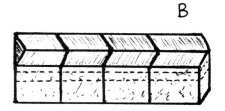

A   Cut out solid wood across grain at an angle
B   lay pieces end to end as shown. A further layer can be
added similarly with the grain oriented the other way. Slice
along the dotted lines to get the thickness required

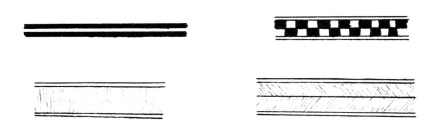

Herringbone banding

Examples of inlays

Fig. 125–7 (*top to bottom*) Fitting the new stringing

Once all this has been done, you can glue the replacement piece in place, making sure it is cramped lightly to hold it there as it dries. On corners or curved edges a combination of masking-tape and clamps can be used. You can also use cotton, old inner tubes, softwood blocks or anything else so long as you ensure that the wood is not scarred (Figs. 125–7). The following day, finish off by lightly sanding in as necessary for an exact fit, then colour and polish as required.

16 Finishing: Cleaning and Staining

Preliminary

Wood finishing encompasses many operations – from cleaning, through colouring and staining, to applying the final coat of wax or polish. Some cases will need only minimal cleaning, some will need their repairs coloured or stained to blend them in. (The difference between 'colouring' and 'staining' is defined below.) Others may even need complete stripping. How does one decide which is best for a case?

The first thing to do is to check what cleaning will do on its own. You do this by using a piece of paper towel, dampened with water, to rub an unobtrusive part of the case. If the towel comes up brown or black, obviously the case is dirty and will need cleaning before going any further. If this happens, before you attempt to clean the whole case down decide whether or not it (or parts of it) will need to be stripped.

TO STRIP OR NOT TO STRIP?

Many purists will tell you that nothing antique should ever be stripped because stripping can drastically reduce value. Solid pine clock cases (mainly thirty-hour) in particular are believed frequently to have been painted when new (and that means painted, not merely varnished) and the modern 'stripped pine' finish is an appeal to sentiment rather than history, though it would probably be difficult to find a restorer who would paint one for you. On the other hand, very few are now painted, and it would be difficult to re-paint one with any confidence if, like most, it had scant evidence of painting extant. So stripping a simple pine case may well be reasonable. With more imposing clocks, the general rule is that stripping will reduce value, but there are times when it is a necessary evil in the course of restoration.

As with repairs, examine the case very closely. If you are planning major repairs to an area, particularly something like removing large areas of veneer with a heat-gun, you may need to strip the finish, but, on the whole, stripping should be done relatively rarely. A clock case does not have to stand up to the same abuse as does, for example, a table or a chair, and as a rule stripping is necessary only if the finish has completely perished. A perished finish shows large patches of bare wood, flaking polish or severe discoloration. Water-marks in the finish perhaps made by rain from an open window can often be removed with a fine abrasive and are not necessarily grounds for stripping. Iron stains, usually caused by nails and characterized by their grey-black colour, will require stripping if they are very disfiguring, because their treatment means going back to the bare wood. The procedure for stripping is outlined below.

Cleaning

The key to cleaning is always to start with the mildest approach and to work up the scale as required, because otherwise you might strip or over-clean the surface inadvertently. People generally prefer their antiques to look old, not as if they have just been made, so in cleaning it is as well always to err on the side of caution. With practice and a good eye, you will eventually be able to look at a case and know immediately what cleaning method is required.

Stripping is the most severe of cleaning methods, involving harsh solvents and mechanical friction. If you are uncertain, or decide against it, the case must still be cleaned superficially. The great majority of cases received have coats of wax on them, and these need to be removed without taking off the real patina, which is deeper. Wax can be cleaned off with white spirit or a proprietary wax cleaner before you embark.

Fig. 128   Buffing up burnishing cream

Start cleaning with a damp paper towel. If this gives no visible improvement, a little soap can be added in the form of washing-up liquid. If the surface is still sticky, you can again use white spirit in the same way – this will remove wax and grease built up from years of handling. If none of these satisfies, move on to stronger fluids, including ammonia, methylated spirits and, finally, stripper. Any of these cleaners can be assisted by additional friction with abrasives, starting with fine rottenstone, moving up through pumice (various grades) and steel wool (moving from very fine through to coarse). Note, however, that abrasive paper is not used on its own in any part of the cleaning process. When you are using fluids, always wipe them off immediately.

There are not many short-cuts in antiques restoration, but with cleaning there is almost a panacea – burnishing cream (obtainable only from a specialist wood-finish supplier). In essence, it is a very fine abrasive suspended in liquid, and it simultaneously cleans and polishes. As its name suggests, burnishing cream gives a very high (glossy) finish which is not always desirable. It is as well to test it on a small out-of-the-way piece to see if the result will be acceptable. It is applied with a paper towel, leaving it for a few minutes to dry, and then buffing it off with a soft cloth (Fig. 128).

Stripping

For stripping you will need a quantity of commercial stripper (one suitable for varnishes and polishes), a working container, an old brush, some coarse steel wool and some newspaper. You will also require rubber gloves and an overall. Stripping is a very messy business and strippers are harmful to the skin.

Lay the newspaper out under and around the area to be stripped, masking any parts you want to retain (Fig. 129). Where keys or handles have been removed, stuff the holes with tissue paper to prevent stripper from falling through, and pour a small quantity of stripper into your tin or container – more can always be added later as you need it, but too much cannot be put back.

Using the brush, stipple a fairly thick coating on to the area which you want to strip. Make sure that you do not cover much more than a square foot at first, as you will find it impossible to stop the stripper drying out over a larger area. Leave the stripper for a little while to do its work – this may be almost immediate or it may take several minutes. Watch for a bubbling or pickling action to start. If the stripper starts to dry out before this happens, apply more – the stripper is supposed to do the work, not you! When the pickling starts, clean off the sludge with a pad of coarse steel-wool, making sure that you go in the direction of the grain to avoid scarring the wood. If huge quantities of old polish are clogging up the steel-wool straight away, use a scraper, but it must be fairly soft and blunt (a plastic applicator for glue or filler or a piece of stiff card will do – Fig. 130). Move on to the next area and repeat the process.

When you have covered the whole area which you want stripped, go back over it again – it may take several applications to remove all the finish. When the wood is completely bare, neutralize (with the method suggested on the can) any stripper that may have been left in the grain. Applying methylated spirits on a pad of very fine steel-wool is one method of doing this. The wood is then ready for refinishing, staining, or whatever is required.

Fig. 129   Masking around an area to be stripped

Fig. 130   Scrape stripping

Staining and Colouring

If you have had to replace any veneers or wood, as we had to do with the Burgess case, you will need to stain and colour them to blend in. While the two terms are often used as if they were interchangeable, it is worth distinguishing them. As we use it, 'staining' means the application of various different substances to bare wood to give a base colour. They always soak into and react with the wood. 'Colouring', on the other hand, denotes the application of colour on top of some form of sealer, usually as a means of disguising the glue-line or just for completing the blending process. Note that (rather confusingly) one can use stains for colouring as well as for actual staining.

Stains come in various forms: chemical (where they react with chemicals present in the wood to create a new colour), spirit, oil, and water-based. Only oil and water-based are really of much use to the amateur. There is a surprising amount of uncertainty about the types of stain and their uses, but the differences are important. It is all too easy to pick a can of stain off the shelf simply for its colour and regardless of type, so the differences are summarized below.

OIL-BASED STAINS

Oil-based stains are available from specialist suppliers or, in their naptha form, from DIY stores. They are slow drying and thus very easy for the inexperienced to work with. They stain well, and can enhance the figure of the wood by emphasizing grain contrasts. They can be mixed easily to give different shades. Their primary disadvantage is that they prevent the use of water-based systems afterwards. Secondly, unlike water stains, they cannot generally be used again to deepen the colour, and they are not good for subtle mixing of shades.

CHEMICAL STAINS

These are normally supplied in a powder form, to be mixed with water for application. Their biggest advantage is that they react with chemicals already present in the wood and so are absolutely permanent, showing very little tendency to fade even in strong sunlight. Unfortunately, their disadvantages far outweigh their advantages. Because they are applied with water, they raise the grain, making it impossible to tell what effect they will have until the wood has dried out completely. And they can give extremely inconsistent results, even across just one panel, since they are reliant on substances in the wood to activate them. They are best left in the hands of an expert.

SPIRIT STAINS

Like oil stains, these generally come already made up in solution, but from specialist suppliers only. They are generally unsuitable for use on antique clock cases because they are carcinogenic, very difficult to apply well, and prone to extreme colour changes on exposure to sunlight (the red, for example, turns green!).

WATER STAINS

Water-based stains can be obtained only from specialist suppliers. They are the least fugitive of all the stains – i.e. they fade at a much slower rate on exposure to light. They are easy to work with (albeit slightly more tricky than oil-based), and are relatively quick drying, which means that several coats can be applied in one day. They are very easily intermixed and diluted, giving almost an infinite range of colours. They do not reject other parts of the finishing process, and since they are water based there is no fire or inhalation risk. Their biggest disadvantage is that they raise the grain of the wood and this requires extra, pre-emptive preparation.

RAISING THE GRAIN

As the water in the stain is absorbed into the cells of the wood it makes the grain swell, creating a rough or 'furry' feel. Account must be taken of this in applying water stains. To produce the effect, take a scrap piece of new hardwood and sand it progressively, starting with 80 grit paper, through 150 grit and finishing up with 320 grit, making sure that you always sand with the grain. Now feel the surface. It should feel beautifully smooth. Apply a damp cloth to it, imitating the effect of stain. Leave it to dry and then feel the wood again. It will feel rough and hairy; but if you sand it again now, with just the 320 grit paper and going diagonally across the grain, it will feel smoother than ever. This whole process, anticipating the effect of the stain, is called 'raising the grain', and must be carried out with clean water before using any water stain on bare wood. Otherwise you will be left with a patchy and rough finish.

RECOMMENDED STAIN

In practice we would strongly recommend using water stains because of their superb mixing ability. They are also cheaper than oil stains. It will mean 'raising the grain' first on bare woods, but the result is worth the extra work. Water stains can be bought in powder form (where you mix them to the strength and colour required), or in pre-mixed cans. The cans usually work out cheaper. They are just as good as the powder and can as easily be mixed with other colours.

VANDYKE BROWN

This is really part of the water-stain family and is the miracle of finishing, just as burnishing cream is the magic agent of cleaning. It can be bought as crystals or powder and is used as a brown stain or (as we shall see) as a way of 'dirtying' or 'antiquing' repairs to make them almost invisible.

Applying Water Stains

After raising the grain as described, stain should be applied to bare wood with brush or rag, working quickly and evenly along the grain. Try to stain in strips rather than blocks (see Fig. 131) or you may find you get overlapping lines which cut across the grain and are impossible to disguise.

While the stain is still damp, go over it with a dry cloth or paper towel. This helps to even out any overlaps or runs.

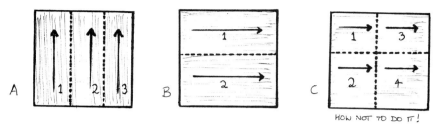

Fig. 131   Applying water stains. Avoid drying lines between sections by keeping wet and working fast. Avoid dry lines across the grain (as in C) at all costs. Brush with the grain if at all possible

Leave the stain to dry for about half an hour and then see if you are happy with the colour. To check what colour the wood will have when polished, wipe it with a thin coat of methylated spirits which, while wet, will show what colour the wood will have under a clear polish. Water-staining can be repeated as required to deepen the colour. When you are quite happy with the colour reached, leave the piece at least ovenight to dry before going on to the next stage.

Filling the Grain

We use staining to bring our wood to the correct colour, but this will not help it to blend so that it looks part of the original piece. The next stage towards this objective is to fill the grain.

STOPPING WAX

If you are trying to touch in only a small repair, you can use stopping wax to fill the grain. This can be bought in various shades or you can make your own (see Appendix). To apply, rub the wax over the area which you want filled, and take off the excess with a cloth. This will leave wax filling up the pores in the wood, saving considerable time, effort and expense when you come to the polishing stage. If you do not have the exact shade of stopping wax required, use one slightly darker rather than lighter.

SANDING SEALER

Using stopping wax is too laborious for large surfaces, such as a panel. For these it is easier to use a sanding sealer. This is a shellac-based liquid, which is very thick in comparison to the normal shellac polish. Apply it according to the instructions. Usually this means brushing it on in line with the grain. Care is needed when brushing it on, because it dries very fast and you will not be able to go back over each brush stroke.

Sanding sealer acts in exactly the same way as stopping wax; it drops into the pores of the wood, effectively filling and sealing them, thus saving time and expense at a later stage. You will probably need several coats, and each one should be left to dry before sanding down with 320 grit Silicon Carbide paper. This is used in preference to garnet paper because it contains a dry lubricant which helps to prevent clogging. As you sand the sealer you will generate quantities of white dust which will drop into the grain, showing if more coats are needed. When sanding, take care not to rub completely through the sealer or you will remove the stain from the wood below. Edges and corners are particularly at risk here.

Proprietary grain fillers are also available. They can be used in place of a sealer, but application is more tricky and prone to errors. For the amateur, sealer is the best method.

Oak is generally left with quite a lot of grain showing, since this looks more natural, while mahogany is usually filled almost completely. These customs display the figure of the wood to best advantage. Finally, you will need to give the work a quick wipe of polish with your rubber (see Chapter 17), and then leave the piece to dry off completely, usually overnight, before moving to the colouring stage.

Colouring

Colouring involves a combination of several different techniques to obtain the final result. For example, water stains can be 'floated' on the polished surface to add a slight tint overall. If this is done, it is imperative that they are left to dry out completely before 'fixing' with a wipe of shellac polish.

Vandyke brown is particularly useful at this stage as it can be used very thickly, applied with a rag (to simulate dirt perhaps), or thinly as a colour wash. To use it, wet a pencil brush and dip it in the powder. Dab the brush

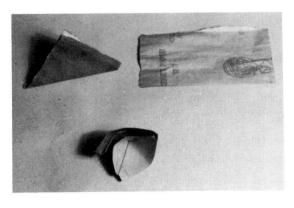

Fig. 132   Containers for colouring

Figs. 133 & 134   Blending in the grain

on a piece of paper – or, even better, a tile or the back of your hand – to dissolve the powder, and add more powder or water as needed to dilute or strengthen the stain.

Disguising glue lines and the edges of patches involves polish and pigments. Start with the lightest colour discernible in the surrounding wood. Make a small cornet out of used abrasive paper or an empty film canister (Fig. 132), and pour in a little polish. Dip a pencil brush into the polish and use the wet brush to pick up a little pigment. Wipe the brush on the edge of the paper (or whatever you have used) to mix in the pigment, and check the strength of the colour. Over the line which you want to disguise, lightly brush the colour in tiny lines, going with the grain (some people even use tiny dots here). This will start to break up the outline of any unwanted line. Continue using other colours, until you are satisfied with the result. Then you will usually need to finish off with a thin coat of Vandyke just to add the final touch. Leave it all to dry, but don't forget to 'fix' it with a couple of coats of polish in the morning.

You may have some difficulty with these techniques if you have not used them before, so practise on scrap wood. However, mistakes can be rectified by wiping with a cloth impregnated with methylated spirits, and the following key points will help: always 'fix' with a little polish between different colours; give water stains plenty of time to dry before trying to fix them; make sure you use very small quantities of pigment at a time (or you will end up with little mounds of colouring which will spoil the effect); remember that you are trying to disguise unwanted lines, not cover them up completely – if you use pigments like a paint to obliterate a line, you can be sure that that is exactly what it will look like!

Finally, after you have finished with the pigments, use a strong mix of Vandyke brown to carefully touch in the missing grain and blend the figuring of the surrounding wood, as shown in Figs. 133–4.

17 Polishing

Some uses of polish have already been mentioned, but we come now to what is generally understood by 'polishing' – namely, the final finish. Many people are apprehensive when they realize that polishing will be necessary. This seems to be due in the main to the 'mystique' which surrounds one technique in particular (i.e. French polishing). However, the vast majority of the longcase clocks, whether solid or veneered, ante-date French polishing, with its rather hard and glossy finish, and do not require it. They benefit rather from a sealer and then a wax finish. For either technique practice is the principal way to overcome difficulties, and it is best to experiment on an off-cut of hardwood or a piece of veneered plywood before trying to polish your clock case itself.

Traditional Wax Polishing

Wax polishing in the traditional way does *not* involve going down to a supermarket and buying a tin of 'Antique Wax', reading the instructions and slapping it on. These tinned waxes are designed for ease of application and as a result they use cheaper blends of waxes as extenders. Experimentation will reveal their drawback. Apply a bit of this wax, following the instructions, to a dining table or coffee table in your living room. After you have left it for the required time and buffed it off as hard as you can, press your thumb into the surface. Not surprisingly, you are left with a thumb-print. This can be rubbed off, but the finish always marks again because the wax is basically too soft to use as a finish.

The remedy is to make your own polish. From your finishing-supplier buy some beeswax and carnauba wax. Melt them together in a double boiler (essential for safety) in equal quantities by weight until they are liquid. Then add a couple of spoonfuls of real turpentine (not white spirit or turpentine substitute). Leave, usually overnight, to cool and set. Whatever container you use for mixing your wax (the economy 'two tin' method in Chapter 12 is recommended), it should be only about half-full when the wax is made.

APPLYING WAX POLISH

To apply the wax you will need a stiff brush, about 2″ (50 mm) wide. You can in fact buy specialist wax-polishing brushes (at a specialist price, of course), but it is cheaper and almost as good to cut down a decorating brush to two-thirds or half its length, this will make it about the right stiffness. Wear an overall – this is a messy business – and read the safety precautions on the turpentine; it can affect your skin and you may need to wear gloves.

To prepare the polish, pour about a teaspoonful of turpentine into the centre of the now solid mixed wax, and stir hard with the brush. You will need to dip the brush lightly in some pigment to add colour to your wax, or you will end up with a white residue in the grain of the wood. Keep stirring hard, adding more turpentine as necessary, until you have a thick paste wax on your brush and on top of the solid wax – then stir some more. This stirring will take at least ten minutes and is hard work, but it is essential for a good polish.

When you feel that the wax is ready, apply it in small circles, say a square foot at a time, over the surface which you want polished. Immediately after covering one small area, use the brush to straighten the wax out in line with the grain. The reason for using small circles first of all is to drive the wax into the grain. Afterwards, quickly wipe off the excess wax with paper towels and leave it to dry. If you don't take off the excess you will be unable to buff to a good finish. While you are waiting for the first area to dry, you can carry on with the rest until you have covered the whole panel in a similar way. Once it has all been left to dry (for about twenty minutes), buff it off with a clean soft rag. After two coats you should see a beautiful smooth surface which looks shiny, but not hard and glossy, and feels lovely and silky. The case (and you) will smell of beeswax and turpentine. After doing all this – and the results are worth it – you can see why mass manufacturers make their waxes softer and easier to apply; on the other hand, the finish on your case will be much more durable.

A short historical note here: authentic finishing using exactly the same methods as originally used would exclude the use of a sealer. The original finish would have been either all wax, or else a kind of varnish which over the years would have worn away and been replaced by wax to give the desirable patina that results from years of hand waxing. If you wish to follow this method, it will take an extremely long time (remember that the patina has been built up over two hundred years) and effort. The use of sealers or grain fillers reduces this period to a minimum and still produces acceptable results.

Shellac (French) Polishing

French polish normally will be appropriate on clocks of a later date which have been finished this way before. The existing finish will be bright and hard and may be crazed. French polish also was often used as a basis for wax polishes. Relatively few longcase clock cases were French polished completely in the manner of, say, a table or a piano.

To apply shellac polish, either as a finish in itself or simply to fix a colour or pigment when disguising patches, we need to make a special polishing pad. This is called a 'rubber' or 'fad'. To make one you need a square of linen (an old, clean cotton handkerchief or piece of cotton sheeting will do) about nine or ten inches (25 cm) square, and a piece of wadding the same size. Fold the wadding into a kite shape and then fiddle it into a pear shape with a definite point at one end. Place the shaped wadding on the square of linen, and pick it up and hold from underneath (see Fig. 135 a–i). Fold the linen so that it creases at the point of the wadding and then, starting at this point, fold and twist the cloth back to form a cord-like shape along the back of the wadding, taking up all the slack fabric. As you get to the end of the pad, you will have a little excess; fold this up so that it snuggles into your palm. All the time you are making the rubber you must make sure that you maintain the point, because this will get polish into the corners. Try making a rubber a few times without polish so as to master it. It soon becomes a fairly slick procedure.

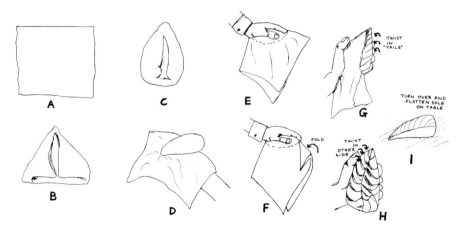

Fig. 135   The stages of making a rubber for polishing (practise several times before you need it!)

The rubber has to be 'charged' with shellac (French polish). Refer to Chapter 12 for details of which polish to use. Charging the rubber entails undoing it all to insert polish. You can peel it back like a banana and apply polish directly to the 'sole' of the wadding. Others advocate opening out the wadding slightly and pouring the polish in the back. Try both and see which you prefer. No set amount of polish can be specified – only experience will tell. If you use too much, you will get lines (the equivalent of runs in paint), but if you use too little the rubber will drag. Be sure to practise on a waste panel first.

BODYING UP

To apply shellac polish you will need good light, preferably daylight. On bare wood the first coat is applied with a firm, circular motion to force it into the grain and seal the surface.

Fig. 136   Bodying up

'Bodying up' comes next – applying a series of straight wipes from one side to another, working with the grain in an unbroken line (Fig. 136). This is done several times, leaving enough time between coats for the polish to dry a bit. On a large surface this means that you can start the next coat immediately. On a small surface you may need to wait a couple of minutes. The time taken for the polish to dry sufficiently for the next coat will vary according to how much polish there is in the rubber, how hard you press, the size of the area, the temperature and the humidity. With all these variables to consider, it is better to leave it for a few minutes rather than risk lifting the previous coat by rushing.

Most polishers tap the sole of the rubber on their hand, or the leg of the workbench, after filling it each time; this helps to spread the polish evenly throughout the rubber and to squeeze out excess polish. If you find that the rubber is leaving lines across the surface but is not dragging, you are probably using too much polish; top it up with just a small amount – you can always add more if necessary. If the rubber drags after several coats, despite having the requisite amount of polish in it, then stop and leave the case overnight to dry before deciding if more polish will be needed.

If something goes wrong with the first 'bodying up' stage and you feel that you will have to rub down the surface, leave it overnight to go completely hard before rubbing down. Otherwise you will end up in a very sticky mess, probably having to strip the surface back down again. If the polish starts to get a whitish mist in it as it is applied, *stop*. Leave it to dry overnight before restarting. This 'bloom' is the result of too much humidity in the air, and the polish must be left to dry right out or else problems will be sealed into the surface. This is obviously more likely to happen in a cold unheated workshop, or on a foggy or misty day. When you leave the panel or panels to dry, don't cover them with a blanket (you will end up with a hairy case!), and don't try to clean off any dust which settles while drying (you could mark the polish).

Gradually build up the surface in this way, adding meths to the rubber a little more each time you fill it so as to dilute the shellac, until eventually you are putting in pure meths and virtually no shellac. Be careful not to add too much meths at once, and keep the rubber moving on the surface or the meths will 'burn' through the polish, leaving it with sticky dull patches. Should this happen, top up the rubber with shellac only, and go back to the bodying up stage. On the rare occasions when this does not work, you will have to leave the polish overnight to dry out. Then the following day you will need to cut it back with Silicon Carbide paper (320 grit) and start bodying up again.

'FIXING' AND SEALING IN COLOURING

For 'fixing' in a colour while disguising repairs, you will need only one swift wipe of polish instead of many coats, though you will need to allow for the fact that you are eventually going to finish off your polishing by cutting back the shellac slightly with steel wool and applying wax, so that the finished result is suitably mellow. Therefore, in 'fixing' apply enough polish so that, in the final stage, you will not cut right through your carefully applied colours and pigments. If you have read about using some sort of oil in the finishing process, ignore this advice. The oil is used only as a lubricant and is not necessary here (particularly as the case-restorer tries to avoid that 'just French polished' look), and it can cause enormous problems if not correctly used.

'PULLING OVER'

The following day, if the surface is very uneven or there is a lot of grain showing, you may need further finishing. This is called 'pulling it over'. It can be done the same day, within an hour or two if necessary (while the shellac is still soft), but the need is usually more apparent the following day when the shellac has sunk into the grain overnight. If you are doing it the following day, put on a couple of coats of polish before starting.

To pull over, dust off the surface and then put a few drops of methylated spirit on to your rubber (which should be virtually exhausted of polish). Start with small circular movements and go over the whole area. The spirits will partly dissolve the polish and lift and move it around. The rubber should not either drag or leave wet marks. You can sometimes see a vapour-trail as the spirits evaporate. Work as quickly as possible and don't let the rubber stop at any point – lift it off the panel at the end of each stroke with a little flourish. Do these circles a couple of times before moving on to small figures-of-eight with the grain (Fig. 137). Repeat with larger figures-of-eight until you are using one figure to cover the whole width of the panel (not forgetting to top up with a little methylated spirit as required). Finish with a couple of wipes in line with the grain. Pulling over may need to be repeated once or twice to produce the required result. Always use the smallest possible amount of spirits – too much will just 'burn' through the surface, undoing all your good work thus far. The same is true if you do not keep the rubber moving all the time.

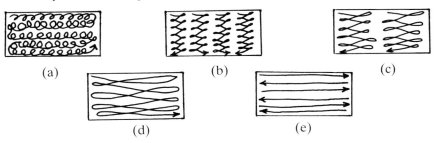

(a)   (b)   (c)

(d)   (e)

Fig. 137   Pulling over

RUBBING DOWN AND WAXING
As already mentioned, the high gloss produced by this method looks false and is undesirable on antique furniture, particularly on clock cases. Leave the polish to harden, preferably over two days, and then go over it with very fine steel wool, following the line of the grain. This will dull it down ready to have a wax polish put on top just to finish it off. Generally, you should try to use as little shellac as possible in the whole process; it is the wax polish which eventually gives an old piece the coveted patina.

18   Odds and Ends

Removal and Refitting of Glass

It is very common for the hood glass to be broken, but it is a relatively simple task to replace it. Glasses are most often fitted with putty, and if the putty has been there for a long time it will be absolutely rock solid. Do not try to chop it out as it is with a chisel or you risk a broken door and butchered fingers. Use a hot-air gun and old chisel to lever it out (Fig. 138). Putty is oil-based and the heat from the gun will force some of the oil still in it to the surface, softening it and making it easier to peel out.

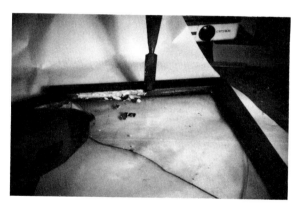

Fig. 138   Removing old putty

When you have removed all the glass, make sure that the rebate in which it lay is clean before you fit new glass. You can cut your own glass, and even for authenticity use an old picture glass, but usually (and particularly in the case of arched doors) it is best to take the door down to a local glass shop and have a glass cut to fit. This is preferable to trying to make an accurate copy, including the rebate, on paper. To fit it in, it is best to use the brown putty rather than the grey, which looks less authentic. Start by lining the rebate with a thin layer. Then place the glass in position on top of this and push down gently. When the glass is bedded evenly you can putty it in, smoothing the putty with a putty knife and fingers. Do not worry about the inevitable fingermarks on the glass – they can be cleaned off later with white spirit. The door can now be left to set. Be careful when refitting the hood; putty remains soft for weeks.

Brass and Gilt Ornament

Most longcase clocks have some brass or gilt brass decorations. These can include the top and bottom of columns (the capitals), handles and escutcheons round locks, and finials. They are usually in a greeny black tarnished state and require cleaning. Remove them from the case and immerse them in the movement-cleaning solution described in Chapter 4, leaving them to soak for several hours. Do not use abrasives before soaking them. If there is any gilding on the brass, abrasives will remove it and this is to be avoided at all costs. In fact, where the gilding is clearly a feature, do not treat the pieces with the ammonia solution but merely brush them with hot water and soap. After soaking, take them out, brush them with a soft old toothbrush and rinse them off in water. If they are not gilded, you can use fine steel wool and burnishing cream to bring them up. It will depend on the quality and value of the clock whether you treat gilded pieces with many of the substitutes (notably 'gold' wax) available at an art shop or have them professionally re-gilt.

DISTRESSING BRIGHT BRASS

Missing finials can be replaced from specialist suppliers, as can escutcheons, hinges, etc. However, they tend to come with a polished finish that immediately shouts that they are new. A mild distressing can be carried out with steel wool, though this tends to look rather artificial. It is better to use a pickling box that requires some preparation.

You need a plastic box with a sealable lid, some shredded newspaper, sawdust and ammonia. Put the newspaper and the sawdust in the box, pour a little ammonia over them, seal and shake up. Leave this for a week or so. Then the paper will have turned brown and the whole lot will look rather

Fig. 139   New and distressed brass

like garden compost, but with the characteristic smell of ammonia. Put in the brass and leave for a few hours, checking periodically on its colour, which progresses to a greenish-blue. Remove the pieces and clean with a brass brush (suede shoe-brush) or very fine steel wool. Fig. 139 shows a new hinge before and after treatment in this way. You can, of course, remove the object before so drastic a change has taken place.

Locks

There is normally only one lock on a longcase, that on the trunk door. If this is lacking a key you can buy blanks and try to make your own keys, after dismantling the lock to gauge the dimensions. However, it may be better to consult your local locksmith as to whether the lock can be saved. Replacement locks are available from cabinet-makers' suppliers but nearly always need some work on the case to make them fit.

'Security' devices exist in great variety. The principle is generally to make the hood door openable only when the trunk door, which can be locked, is open. Sometimes this requires a manual bolting of the hood door from inside, and sometimes it is achieved by various levers and catches automatically, the hood door being fastened by the closing of the trunk door. The arrangements are too various to describe here and will usually be clear from examination; a slot or hoop in the lower rail of the hood door indicates that such a mechanism once existed. It must be said that nowadays these barricades are not entirely convenient and one might think twice before restoring them.

Ebonizing

While some early longcase clocks were made with a real ebony veneer, a far greater number are to be found with an 'ebonized' finish, whether it be the whole case or just a part (such as the base of the pilasters on the Scott case). True ebonizing is a complex process involving the use of various chemicals, pigments and even inks. A short cut is to use a black (French) polish as an alternative. Apply it with a brush or rubber, leaving it overnight to dry before cutting back with 320 grit Silicon Carbide paper. Then apply another coat. When you are satisfied with the result, rub down hard with fine steel wool and wax before buffing off with a soft cloth. Otherwise it will look shiny and false.

Part IV   Variations

The following pages outline some of the commoner types of mechanism found on longcase clocks over nearly two hundred years. It should not be assumed that they are necessarily any rarer than alternatives found in the two example clocks. If you are faced with one of these variations, it would be as well to read first the relevant main section in the book before trying to follow the other mechanism closely.

   Variations are arranged alphabetically in two groups, as follows:

Thirty-hour Clocks

— Countwheels
— Duration between windings
— Letting off the striking
— Moonwork and datework (thirty-hour and eight-day)
— Pendulums
— Posted movements
— Rope drive
— Single-handed clocks
— Thirty-hour ratchets
— Three-wheel trains

Eight-day Clocks

— Dead-beat escapement
— Duration between windings
— Internal countwheels
— Pin-locking for striking
— Repeating devices

Thirty-hour Clocks

Countwheels (see Chapter 7)

The type of countwheel on the Burgess clock – a flat disc with square slots to indicate the locking points – is by far the commonest on thirty-hour clocks and, indeed, on countwheel clocks generally. However, there are two other types which are by no means uncommon and occur mainly in the later eighteenth century. These are the 'projecting section' and the 'pinned' types.

In the first type the usual raised sections are instead riveted into the wheel at right-angles, projecting forwards or backwards. Operation is the same as with the flat type. Generally the edge of the countwheel itself is toothed and replaces the commoner type's attached gearwheel. Economy in the saving of a wheel was probably the reason for this development.

In the pinned type, projecting pins replace the beginning of each of the conventional slots and a different arrangement is used for locking. The countwheel detent is looped in such a way that it is *raised* by an approaching pin (whereas conventionally the detent *drops* into a slot). Between the plates this brings a blunt-ended locking-piece (on the detent's arbor) into the path of a pin, rather than the hoop of the more usual form of locking wheel. This therefore means that these trains lock when the detent is up, whereas the normal ones lock when the detent is down. Here again the countwheel itself is toothed and there is no attached wheel to mesh with the greatwheel's pinion. This was clearly an economical arrangement.

In addition, the usual flat countwheel is sometimes found with a slope beginning each raised section. Whereas normally the sloped shape of the locking-piece acting on the hoop edge raises the detent, in this modified type the lift is given outside, by the detent's riding up the slope, and the locking-piece tip can be square; pin-locking (described above) is used also with this kind of wheel.

Finally, there is another, less common, type of external countwheel. This has raised nibs jutting out from the circumference, and no slots. The nibs are short, like pins, but cut out of the brass blank, and the working is as with the pin countwheel but with the nibs or 'pins' being radial outwards and the train locking when the locking-piece is raised against the pin in the locking wheel. The detent moves a very short distance and this type is subject to wear and difficult to adjust.

With the 'pin' and 'nib' versions it is common to resort to 'single arbor' practice, with all the striking levers being mounted on one arbor for preset rigidity and also for economy. Generally, this occurs towards the end of the longcase period, but one example has been seen with a conventional countwheel, single arbor, dating from about 1705. This was done by using a lifting/warning-piece (through the plate) pivoted freely on the main locking/detent arbor, with a link-piece so that the lifting-piece raised the locking, which stayed up when the lifting-piece fell at the hour. Here also the minute wheel was placed unusually below the cannon pinion to which the lifting pin was fitted (see below, 'Letting Off Thirty-Hour Striking').

Duration between Windings

Your clock may not run for a full thirty hours, but if it does not go for well over twenty-four hours then either the chain/rope is too short or the case is too short (or both) and may not belong with the movement.

The duration is determined by the greatwheel gearing, subject to the chain or line. The length of the pendulum has nothing to do with the duration of running, which is set by the wheel or wheels in the train before the hands and by the line.

New chains and ropes are always full-length and often need to be shortened. They should be no longer than for the weight, just to avoid touching the ground when the clock is fully unwound and the counter-weight up against the seatboard. If they are longer, they can slip off the pulleys. Where the case seems too short, a small extension may be available by changing to a shorter weight or a squatter pulley. Note that rope-driven clocks will run short if too thick ropes are used; the rope rides on the pulley flanges where it is inclined to slip and where it is effectively driving a larger pulley. This can cause loss of some two hours between windings.

Although occasional conversions were made in the past, it should be seen as impossible to convert a thirty-hour clock to run for eight days. Such gross modification as to amount to vandalism would be involved. The high cost would be an additional deterrent. This is because there is never room between the plates for the necessary wheels. Any such clock would be divested of whatever value it has as an antique – that is, if you could find anyone prepared to undertake the work. There are good reasons why – despite practice in some reproduction clocks – eight-day movements with their heavier weights are key-wound and would require holes to be drilled in the dial. Many good thirty-hour brass dials have of course been butchered in this way to replace unwanted painted dials in eight-day clocks. They are usually obvious from poor centring of the holes, mutilation of the frontplate or a falseplate for fitting, and winding holes cut out from engraved ornament.

As there is the slight possibility that you may have acquired an altered lantern-clock fitted, possibly two centuries ago, into a longcase, it should be added that lantern clocks (which have posted movements and show holes for hanging side doors) may run for twelve hours or even less and may have separate lines and chains for each train. If this appears to be the situation, it would be best to consult a specialist about any work on the clock.

Letting off Thirty-hour Striking (see Figs. 140 a–d).

The variations here are many, but they basically depend on whether the warning-piece is between plates or out in front, and on whether, when the warning-piece falls for actual striking to occur (rather than the run to warning), the locking-piece also falls or must be held up. (See also above, 'Countwheels'.)

In the Burgess clock the warning-piece is in front, part of the lifting-piece bent round through a slot in the frontplate (as is usual in later plated movements). The lifting-piece is mounted separately, not on an arbor but on a stud in the front plate (Fig. A). It is activated by a pin on the minute-wheel (as in eight-day clocks). There is an external link-piece with the locking, squared on to the extended locking arbor.

Fig. B shows the common late forked combination of warning- and lifting-pieces which was in general use with eight-day rack striking.

On posted, as on many earlier plated, movements the warning-piece is between the plates on the same arbor as the lifting-piece, which is pinned on to its squared end in front (Fig. C). Connection with the locking is made by an internal finger on the locking-piece arbor. This arrangement is found on four-wheel two-handed clocks as well, but then a shorter lifting-piece, not hooked, is operated by a minute-wheel pin (as in Figs. A & B).

Lastly, pin-locking clocks (see above, 'Countwheels') could place warning-piece, locking-piece and countwheel detent all on the same arbor because – unlike all the arrangements above – their trains start running when these pieces, with the lifting-piece, *fall* (rather than rise) as striking begins. This must have been a considerable economy. One wonders, indeed, whether it might have become the commoner system had countwheel longcase clocks continued to be made.

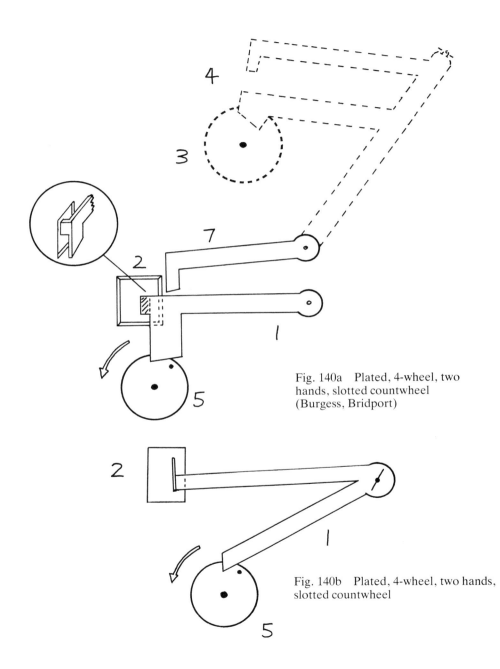

Fig. 140a   Plated, 4-wheel, two
hands, slotted countwheel
(Burgess, Bridport)

Fig. 140b   Plated, 4-wheel, two hands,
slotted countwheel

Fig. 140c Three-wheel, single-handed, slotted countwheel, may be posted

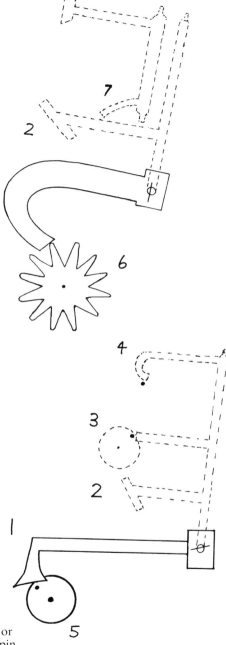

1 Lifting piece raised by minute wheel (4-wheel clocks) or hour starwheel (3-wheel clocks), on stud or on the warning piece arbor
2 Warning piece either behind front plate on lifting piece arbor, or part of lifting piece and bent through a slot in the plate
3 Locking piece or hoopwheel detent
4 Countwheel detent behind back-plate, either on locking arbor or made solid with locking piece and bent through or round plate or pillar
5 Minute motion wheel
6 Starwheel attached to hour wheel in single-handed clocks
7 Link-piece to locking

Fig. 140d Plated or posted, three- or four-wheel, two hands, pin locking, pin countwheel

Thirty-Hour & Eight Day Clocks: Moonwork and Datework Types (see Figs. 141–2 and Chapter 9)

MOONWORK

The connection between the central hour-wheel and some form of lunar disc in both thirty-hour and eight-day clocks shows great variety. Outside London, accuracy and economy (or the best compromise between the two) were pursued with great ingenuity. The usual level of accuracy is to some nine hours in a year which (since for most users the purpose of the dial was to show when there was a chance of a light night) was probably, in practice, quite sufficient. The diagrams show what seem to be the commonest types and are intended to help where moonwork is incomplete. It may well be that there are regional patterns and that types of moonwork could assist in dating and location, but little work has been published on this aspect.

You may – though perhaps not for very long – be interested in following the progress of your clock's moon in relation to what is happening in the sky at night. If so, you need to set it up. The common systems all give variably poor likenesses of the actual appearance of the moon in its phases, so it is difficult just to go out on a clear night and compare. In their weather sections, several newspapers give a diagram of the current state of the moon. Many diaries indicate 'full moon' and 'new moon'. From these indications you can count the current number of days and set by this, rather than the appearance and likeness of the moon.

DATEWORK

We show the commonest types on painted dials and brass dials, but it should be added that on late brass dials there are sometimes found types more usual on painted dials. For all practical purposes it can be said that there is never any mechanical distinction between 31 day, 30 day, 29 day and 28 day months; the indicator has to be moved on by hand in the short months. Sometimes, particularly in brass dials, holes are provided so that the ring can be pushed round with a pin from in front. With painted dials it is often necessary to reach up from the trunk door to turn the date ratchet. This adjustment must not, of course, be made while the mechanism is engaged; the clock will take three to four hours to change the date.

The time of day at which moon and date discs change is controlled by the movable (from inside) twenty-four-hour wheel, if there is one, or fixed (usually at around six o'clock) by the pin in the hour wheel if there is not.

Pendulums

A missing pendulum is not a disaster for a longcase clock. Good standard pendulums are available new from suppliers, or a dealer may be able to provide an old one. The standard pendulum is 1 m long, measuring from

MOONWORK TYPES

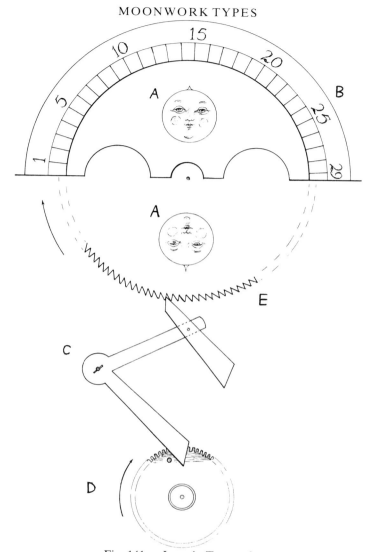

Fig. 141a   In arch, Two-cycle

A   Two full moons, one concealed
B   Age of moon, on arch (as here) or on disc, fixed pointer on arch
C   Deer's foot lever
D   Hour wheel with (day-of-month) pin
E   118 toothed ratchet advanced 12-hourly
     clockwise, one rotation 59 days

An alternative uses a duplicate hour wheel replaced at 2 o'clock, with a pin; replaces deer's foot lever

MOONWORK TYPES

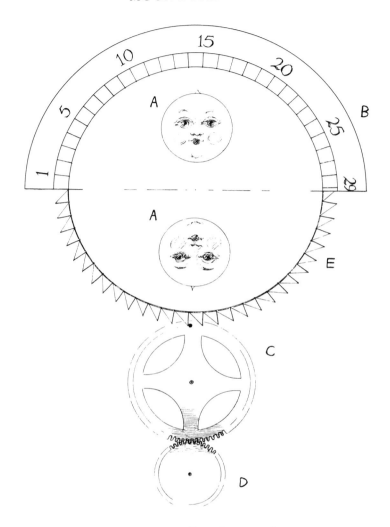

Fig. 141b   In arch, two cycle

A   Two full moons, one concealed
B   Age of moon, on arch (as here) or on disc, fixed pointed on
        arch
C   24-hour wheel with operating pin
D   Hour wheel pinion, geared 1:2 to 24-hour wheel
E   59 tooth ratchet advanced 24-hourly clockwise, one rotation
        59 days

(Indication of age of moon varies as in Fig. 141a)

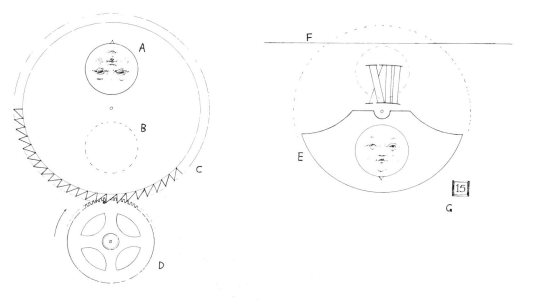

Fig. 141c   Below 12 o'clock on dial, single-cycle

A   Full moon
B   New moon (in fact, background picture)
C   59 toothed ratchet advanced 12-hourly anti-clockwise, one rotation 29 days
D   Hour wheel and operating pin
E   Distinctive aperture (mainly Northern)
F   Edge of dial plate overlapped by disc
G   Optional separate aperture for moon's age

the tip of the suspension to the centre of gravity or (in practice) the centre of the bob. For eight-day clocks this length can be considered universal.

For thirty-hour clocks, however, it is another story – their trains and pendulums vary quite widely, particularly where there is no seconds hand. There is no quick way of knowing whether or not a standard pendulum will do, though a scapewheel count of other than thirty may be an indication. Most often the standard rods can be cut down, but occasionally a new rod has to be made for a longer pendulum.

Where you do not know the length of pendulum required there are two approaches. The first option is to calculate the overall gear ratio (as shown in Chapter 6 – totalling the relevant wheel teeth and dividing by the total of pinion leaves, multiplying the answer by two). The count is carried right through the greatwheel, driving pinion and motion wheel in single-handed clocks. If a standard pendulum beating seconds is involved, the result will

FIG. 142   DAY OF THE MONTH TYPES

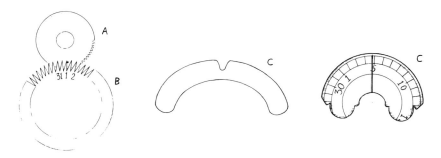

1. Thirty-hour and Eight-day with 'Month'

A   Hour wheel with pin
B   62 toothed ratchet, anti-clockwise, on false plate or dial
C   Common dial aperture shapes, below centre hole

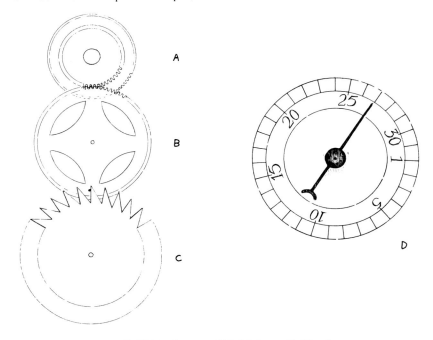

2. Thirty-hour and Eight-day with Hand

A   Hour wheel with large 'pinion'
B   Twenty-four hour wheel geared 2:1 to pinion, having pin to advance ratchet mounted on stud in front plate
C   31 toothed ratchet, clockwise, mounted on dial or false plate
D   Ring marked on dial, hand fitted to ratchet arbor

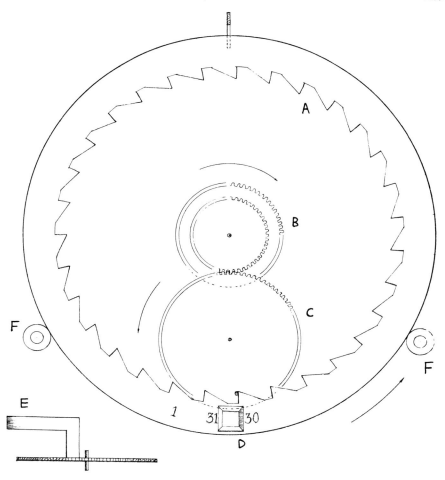

3. Eight-day brass dial

A   31 toothed ratchet, internal teeth, supported behind dial on rollers and top hook
B   Hour wheel and attached large 'pinion'
C   Twenty-four hour wheel geared 2:1 to pinion and having pin or 'flag' to drive ratchet
D   Square aperture above dial's 'VI'
E   'Flag' with cut-out to clear hour snail
F   Supporting hook and rollers attached to back of dial

be 3600 (the number of seconds in an hour). If it is anything else, a modified pendulum is needed. Tables showing the lengths for specified beats per hour will be found in C. Saunier's *Treatise on Modern Horology* (originally 1861, but constantly reprinted and widely available in public libraries), or can be calculated from the formula given in, for example, D. de Carle's *Watch and Clock Encylopaedia* (1950 and reprints).

Those less enamoured by counting wheel teeth may proceed instead by experiment. A temporary pendulum may be made from dowel, with the suspension-spring pinned into a sawn slit at the top, a flat filed to engage the crutch, and a weight movable at the bottom. (You may know from the clock's performance whether your rod needs to be shorter or, exceptionally, longer than standard, since this is how your suspicions about any existing pendulum will have been aroused. If you have no idea, it is simplest to start with a 1 m pendulum extended by a few centimetres). The temporary weight need not be elaborate to give you a guide to the required length – any compact heavy object will suffice if attached by adhesive tape, but it must be heavier than the rod itself. Most pendulums are within a few inches of 39'' (1 m), but examples are found between about 24'' (600 mm) and about 65'' (1.6 m). If you have found the correct length is less than 1 m overall, remember in reducing a new standard rod to allow at least 2'' (5 cm) to take the thread below the bob for regulating. Rods are now normally given a 5BA thread. Notes on the suspension are given in Chapter 6.

Posted Movements

Posted movements, like plated, may be rope or chain driven. As a rule they have three-wheel trains (no seconds hand) and the hand(s) are driven from the pulley greatwheel. But all combinations – single- and two-handed, three or four wheel – are found until well into the nineteenth century. Countwheel striking is all but universal, but occasional rack strikers are known. (Note that, although the term 'three-wheel train' is used, the striking trains are the same as in 'four wheeled' clocks, since greatwheel, hoopwheel, warning wheel and fly are needed in both.) In posted movements the striking train is invariably positioned *behind* the going train, rather than to its right as in thirty-hour plated movements (and to its left in most eight-day movements).

The frame posts may be of square or rectangular iron, or similarly of brass, but the latter were sometimes turned and tapered round, as in many lantern clocks. (The two types of clock are closely related – see above, 'Duration between Windings'.) The various steel arbors for the strike work may be round or square in section. In general, the movements clearly were not polished and a decent cleanliness is sufficient. There are often planishing marks and other disfigurements on the brass top and bottom plates, to which the pillars are normally riveted. From spare screw and other holes in the top plate and centre strip plate, historical changes in the movement may sometimes be reconstructed. For example, it may have been a wall or lantern clock; many of the latter were converted to seconds pendulums in the eighteenth century.

The vertical strip plates have tongues slotting into the bottom plate and are held in place by brass wedges in the top plate. These wedges are often identified by scratch or punch-marks, as they are not always interchangeable. If they are not, it is as well to mark them, front to back. After the invariably huge bell and stiff hammer spring and stop (fixed by nuts in top and bottom plates), the pallets are removed first. They are supported by a small vertical cock at the back, which is screwed to the backplate, and have a long arbor right across the top plate to a riveted bracket at the front. The pallets themselves swing through a hole in the top plate. The firmness of the front cock, and tightness of its pivot hole, should be checked – they often cause trouble.

To dismantle, remove the countwheel and take off its pinion and put it somewhere safe. Then turn to the frontplate and dismantle the motion-work. In these clocks, whether one- or two-handed, the strike lifting-piece is usually pinned to a square arbor carrying the warning-piece between plates. Note carefully the 'clutch' arrangement for setting the hands. This will usually be a stout bowspring, compressed by a pin, working on the main drive pinion, which runs on the going greatwheel arbor. With single-handed clocks, however, this arbor may be squared and the friction drive is incorporated into the big hour wheel with its let-off star-wheel fixed behind it.

You can then take out the frontplate, the going train and the striking arbors, where it will simplify matters if you identify their positions top to bottom with a sketch. The middle plate will be fixed, so you turn the movement round to get access to the striking parts by removing the backplate similarly. (Where, exceptionally, there are four strip plates and diverted arbors, this indicates a lantern clock with original short pendulum and the old verge escapement, the pendulum swinging in the middle of the clock between the centre plates. Consult an expert as to whether this should be restored or the later arrangement retained as an honest part of the movement's history.)

The servicing of these movements (particularly pivots and holes) mainly follows that shown for the plated movement in Part 2. They are very prone to wear and the holes are likely to need considerable attention. This applies especially to the holes for the hammer, with its very stiff spring, and the pallet arbor holes on top. The same is unhappily true of three-wheel train pinions, and you may have to consider replacement of fly and/or scapewheel pinions, for the arbors on these clocks are often tapered and the wheels difficult to move to fresh parts of pinions.

When it comes to re-assembly, start with the striking. It is both essential here and often very difficult to arrange for the hammer tail to be quite free of the pins when striking locks. It can be helpful to wire or otherwise fasten the hammer in position while the other pivots are fitted in, and also to leave fitting of hammer spring and stop till later. Remember also that the warning-wheel must have freedom to run to the warning-piece, so plant it with its pin at the top.

With the pallets mounted on the top plate it is not possible to vary the position of the pallet cock very much in adjusting escapement depth, though fine changes can be made by adding a thin washer or filing down the back cock. It may well be necessary to reface the pallets (see chapter 6).

The threading of chain or rope is easier than on plated movements as the pulleys are more accessible. Here also the greatwheels revolve anti-clockwise; the weight and pulley hang on the left (see Fig. 38).

Posted movements are often not fastened to their seatboards, but sometimes screws are taken up through the board into the bottom plate.

Rope Drive

The first thirty-hour clocks – like lantern clocks, their predecessors – were driven by rope. Chain, however, rapidly caught on, and a movement with rope drive is not necessarily older than one with a chain. Both have their disadvantages; ropes wear and create dust, while chains open up and slip but last longer. Pulley spikes are sharper for ropes. Chain pulleys have a groove down the middle for clearance of the links (Fig. 39). Sometimes one finds a chain on rope pulleys. Such chains are prone to slip and damage the spikes and should be changed – as indeed rope drive may be changed to chains by use of a 'conversion kit' available from suppliers. While a lathe is best for fitting these kits – the holes are made small so that many sizes can be accommodated – it is not essential, since the truth of the pulleys is not absolutely critical.

The main problem with ropes is joining them – the special stranded ropes cannot be spliced like other ropes. Most repairers have their own methods of making a joint which is strong and no thicker than the rest of the rope, and some ways are rather involved. A simple and reliable method is to unravel an inch of each end, to tie a pair of three strands on each side in a reef knot, and to trim the other strands until they come right up to the knot. The joint is then stitched thoroughly with linen or carpet thread, taking in all the loose ends and making sure that much of the stitching goes right through the knot. Finally, roll the joint between the palms of the hands, and trim again.

Joining is often carried out with the rope installed in the movement, and then you must ensure that a) you have the rope correctly round the pulleys, and b) both weight and counter-weight are included in the loops. It is convenient to stick or wire the counter-weight temporarily some way up the loop, away from the joint while it is being made.

Stranded clock rope is readily available from suppliers and no other type (such as sash cords) will do. It comes in some six metric sizes and an old rope will not be a reliable guide to thickness. Measure the pulley between the flanges at the spike tips (most pulleys are misleadingly wide at the outer edge). If in any doubt, buy two sizes or take the pulley to the supplier. While obviously, there is great variation, a new rope usually lasts two to three years. (See also 'Duration' above.)

Single-Handed Clocks

As in the case of rope drive, single-handed clocks persisted long after the minute hand (introduced in the late seventeenth century) had been widely accepted. They were simpler and cheaper and were made throughout the eighteenth century. Domestic time-measurement scarcely demanded accuracy above one quarter of an hour, as shown by dial marking, and in practice the time could actually be read with fair accuracy to within five minutes. The dial and hand must, naturally, match; if there are two hands and a dial with 48 divisions, or one hand and a dial with 60 divisions, the dial (or at least the chapter ring) is suspect – though later addition of a minute hand is possible and some genuine anomalies exist.

The drive and motion-work are different from those of clocks having centre wheels driving minute hands (like the Burgess). The motion-work consists of one large hour wheel, whose pipe bears the single hand and which meshes with a drive pinion, attached to the going greatwheel's arbor. For setting the hands, either this pinion is fitted with a friction spring to the arbor, or the pipe is fastened to the hour wheel by a spring clip located in a slot round its arbor. The single hand has an extended tail for setting to time.

Attached to the hour wheel, and of much the same size, is a twelve-pointed starwheel, used to let off the striking at the hour (see above, 'Letting off the Striking'). It has to be said that these starwheels are not always accurately divided. Moreover, there can be considerable play in the motion-work, so that neither time-showing nor time-sounding is as reliably on the hour as in clocks with a centre wheel. However, some of the trouble is often in a poor fit of the hand and this should be minimized.

The front end of the hour pipe which carries the hand may be rebated so that it pivots in the central hole of the dial. There are two ways of supporting the rear end. Either it is formed into a pivot in the front-plate – in which case the wheel falls out when the dial is removed – or it is hollow and rides on a long central stud which is screwed or riveted into the frontplate. The wheel then stays in place when the dial is removed. This is a better arrangement from several points of view.

While on two-handed clocks the striking is let off by a small lifting-piece raised and let fall by a pin on the oblique minute wheel, on a single-handed clock the lifting-piece has to reach across the front to the central starwheel. These pieces are usually steel and resemble an axe or scythe in shape, though other forms are found. The hooked shape is necessary, of course, because here the letting-off wheel (the starwheel) revolves clockwise, whereas when the minute motion wheel lets off it revolves anti-clockwise and has merely to raise the straight lifting-piece.

Thirty-Hour Ratchets

Several forms of ratchet are found acting on the spokes ('crossings') of the strike greatwheel or on a ratchet wheel (Fig. 52–3). The one on the Burgess clock consists of a pivoted pawl or 'click', kept in place by a leaf spring (see Fig. 51d) Sometimes the spring needs to be bent more tightly or replaced. This entails dismantling the pulley and riveting in place a new slip of hammer-hardened brass, but it was not necessary here. Where the pivoted pawl works on the crossings (rather than on a distinct ratchet wheel) the wear on the spokes is still relatively slight. This type is also used in modern 'chain conversion' kits.

By far the commonest arrangement, at least in the eighteenth century, consists of a circular spring, riveted to the pulley and with a raised edge pressing up against the crossings. Here the rivets often need tightening and the spring may be broken near them. For repair, there is little alternative to filing up a new spring, either in one piece or with the ledge riveted or soldered in place. Brazing a broken spring is unsatisfactory since it weakens the spring.

This type can cause heavy wear on the wheel crossings. Sometimes it may be necessary to solder shaped strips of brass onto the spokes to restore their level. The winding action is inclined at best to be noisy and jerky and, all in all, it is hard to see grounds other than simple economy to explain why this form of ratchet was almost universally used.

It is difficult to establish the history of the different types. The spring type is certainly the older, but other types were in use in the eighteenth century. A lantern clock is known where the main train ratchet is of the spring type but the alarm train uses the pivoted type, both seeming to be original.

Three-Wheel Trains

'Three-wheel' refers to the going train; the striking is the same as on a four-wheel clock – greatwheel, hoopwheel, warning wheel and fly. Three-wheel trains were cheaper than four-wheel. They did not allow of a seconds hand (since the scapewheel, to whose arbor it would be attached, ran anti-clockwise) but they seem to be as often two-handed as single-handed. The pinions wear badly in three-wheel trains, since the gear ratios are higher.

The three-wheel train does not have a centre wheel and therefore its hand(s) are driven from a pinion attached to the greatwheel arbor outside the frontplate. This simply drove a large central hour-wheel in the single-handed clock, but in the two-handed clock special motion work was used which consisted of an extension of the single-handed arrangement. To the drive pinion was fitted a drive wheel. The pinion drove the large hour wheel while through the latter's pipe ran the tube of a 'cannon pinion', a small wheel on a finer pipe, which carried the minute hand and also a pin for letting off the striking. This was driven by a wheel attached to the drive pinion and on the same arbor. The greatwheel arbor usually revolved once in about two hours, so the hour wheel was related to the pinion typically 1:6, with the hour revolving in twelve hours. The drive wheel and minute wheel would be related 2:1, so that the cannon pinion revolved in one hour. Thus the greatwheel arbor drove one unit (the cannon pinion) faster than itself and one unit (the hour wheel) more slowly than itself.

The ratio of drive wheel to cannon pinion has, of course, to be taken into account in calculating the going train of such a clock. Typical counts are drive pinion 12, hour wheel 72; drive wheel 56, cannon pinion 28. For the hour and minute hand to run concentric, the two pairs had to be of identical total size (in this case 84 teeth), a requirement in all motion-work which very much restricts the choice of ratios available.

Eight-day Clocks

Dead Beat Escapements

The vast majority of clocks were fitted with the 'recoil' escapement, so called (as we have seen in Chapter 6) because the pallets are designed to press each scapewheel tooth backwards slightly at each vibration – which you can see if there is a seconds hand. The merit of this was that it limited the swing of the pendulum so that the bob did not hit the sides of a narrow trunk. This created a small arc which made for better timekeeping. Recoil did, however, add to friction in the escapement, causing wear in the scapewheel pinion.

Some better-class clocks were fitted with a dead beat escapement, in which there is no recoil. It was used particularly where a central seconds hand swept the dial and seemingly accurate seconds were needed. The dead beat pallets have separate locking and impulse faces. The wheel teeth lock on the 'corner' of each pallet and the wheel faces the other way, with the radial rather than the sloped part of the tooth leading and engaging

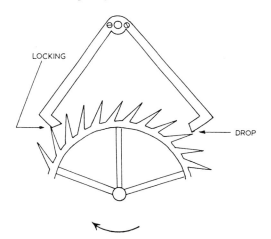

Alternative shape of wheel tooth

Fig. 143   Dead beat escapement

216

(Fig. 143). The locking face is shaped in the circumference of a circle drawn from the pallet arbor. As a result, the tooth does not move forwards or backwards while locked by the moving pallet.

The arc of vibration is very small and the escapement is precision designed and made, the pallets being glass-hard or fitted with jewel stones to prevent wear. As a result, repairs within the amateur's scope are somewhat limited. The pallets are polished with the burnisher but must be re-made or probably replaced if they are worn. The fine scapewheel teeth often need carefully straightening with pliers, but the radial faces must not be filed. The 'drop' is adjusted very finely, as with the recoil escapement (Chapter 6). The commonest fault is 'mislocking', where the pallet strikes an impulse rather than a locking face; this is cured by carefully heating the pallet arms and slightly closing them.

Where there is a centre seconds hand the escapement is placed low, quite near the central arbor, and there are corresponding complications in the train. Quite often these dead beat escapements have been replaced by recoil, the pallets and possibly also the scapewheel being changed. From the point of view of preserving the history of the clock it may be a mistake to convert back to dead beat but, if it is done, this is work for a professional clockmaker, as great accuracy is important and a good finish is usually required on this class of clock.

Duration between Windings

Eight-day clocks run for a week, with a little bit more to allow for convenient regular winding. The size of that bit varies. The clock is fully wound when all the grooves on the barrel are full. They should not be over-full (which the height of the case may sometimes permit), since then coils of line can come off the barrel, wind round the arbor and stop the clock. These coils can be very difficult to extricate, should that happen. (For the same reason, try always to unwind the lines completely, by manipulating the ratchet clicks, before transporting a longcase movement.)

Short running tends to indicate a 'married' or shortened case. Usually evident from the shortness of the plinth, reduction was not uncommon when ceilings were low and plinths tended to rot and split. It will be seen that not all the coils have left the barrel when the weight reaches the ground. The cures are radical and probably unethical; the case can be rebuilt or a smaller barrel (holding more turns of the same line), can be substituted. Shorter weights may help a little. Generally, short duration is best accepted.

Sometimes the barrel can be filled but the weight is not near the ground when unwound. (It should not be *on* the ground, as this may allow the weight to come off its pulley.) This again may indicate a changed case, but not necessarily, because it seems that many clocks were made so that the

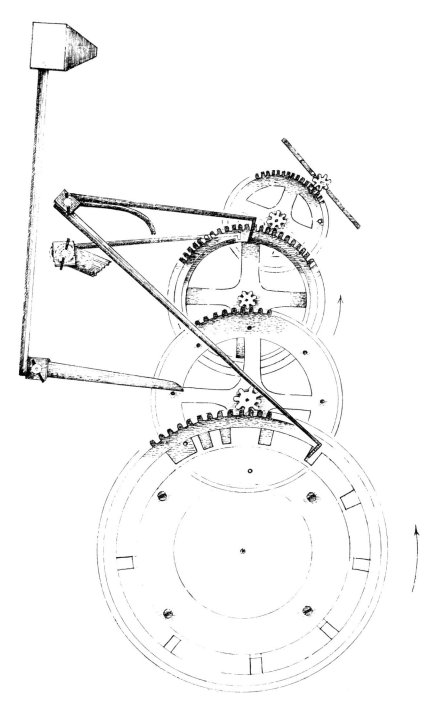

Fig. 144   Internal countwheel striking

clock was fully wound (the coils on the barrel) when the weight was just disappearing from the trunk aperture, rather than meeting the seatboard. (The latter produces an undesirable collision and complicates removal of the weights for any reason.)

In the face of all this, the best course with a restored or newly acquired clock is to establish the position of the weights when all the barrel grooves are full (or space occupied on an ungrooved barrel) and take this as a starting-point before cutting and knotting the lines.

It is never good to have a rack-striking train run out before the going – the going continues to release the lifting-piece and rack, whose tail eventually fouls the snail at 12.00 o'clock. The clock will then probably stop, although it is provided with a springy rack tail to protect it.

Internal Countwheels

Although the countwheel striking system (see Chapter 7) was used throughout the life of the thirty-hour clock, its application to eight-day clocks was limited mainly to the seventeenth and early eighteenth centuries. There were some early clocks with external countwheels but the internal form is the commonest. It is easily recognized by the large notched disc attached to the striking greatwheel and distanced from it by small collets.

The mechanism (see Fig. 144) is very reliable, being basically the same as that of external countwheels in thirty-hour clocks, although the arrangement of the levers is different. Remember, as always with countwheel striking, that the countwheel determines only where the train can be locked; the locking itself is always done by another wheel, which carries an interrupted 'hoop' capable of arresting a floating locking-piece. Above this comes the usual warning-wheel, but the warning-piece is more reminiscent of old thirty-hour clocks again, being internal rather than through the frontplate. Similarly, an extension on its arbor raises the combined locking-piece and countwheel detent, the latter descending in a long sweep to the countwheel below.

There is one special problem in servicing these movements. Their assembly follows the principles for any countwheel system, and these are set out in Chapter 7, but, because the countwheel here is a fixture to the greatwheel between plates, there is no way of adjusting it once the movement is assembled. You have, therefore, to assemble with the locking-piece resting in the hoop gap, the countwheel in a slot on the countwheel, and the hammer tail clear of the hammer pins. If it is not right, the top plate will have to be lifted and the wheel moved.

Pin-Locking

By far the commonest way to lock the rack-striking train was (as in Chapter 8) to have a pin on the gathered rack obstruct a long-tailed gathering pallet. This, of course, occurred outside the movement and in front. The wheel on whose arbor the pallet rides is called the 'locking-wheel', although here it does not itself take part in the locking. (Pin-locking was also used in thirty-hour clocks, replacing the usual hoop, and requiring an upward movement of the countwheel detent to dictate locking. See above. 'Countwheels'.)

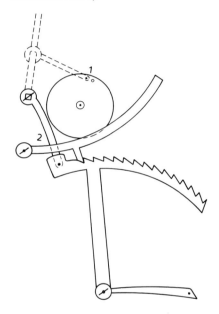

Fig. 145   Pin locking with rack striking
1   Locking piece
2   Locking lever

Note: This is a later, mainly Northern type. Earlier practice was to have the rack slot for the rack-hook cut very deep so that the hook fell further to drop and lock, having on its arbor a locking-piece between plates

An alternative, however, was to lock on a pin protruding from this wheel (see Fig. 145). This seems to have been mainly a Northern practice. Locking then occurred between the plates. A finger or detent was pivoted on an arbor so that it could move into the path of the locking-wheel pin. This had to be operated by the gathering rack, and so the detent arbor was extended through the plate into a square, on which was mounted another, angled, finger which was moved by the usual pin in the rack.

It is a simple and reliable method but it complicates assembly. With the 'ordinary' rack movement you usually can arrange for the train to lock only when the hammer is free of hammer (pin-wheel) pins – as is essential – by changing the position of the gathering pallet on its arbor. With pin-locking, you cannot do this, since the locking-wheel with its pin cannot be moved round on its arbor. Therefore, when assembling the movement you must

Fig. 146   Simple Repeat Devices

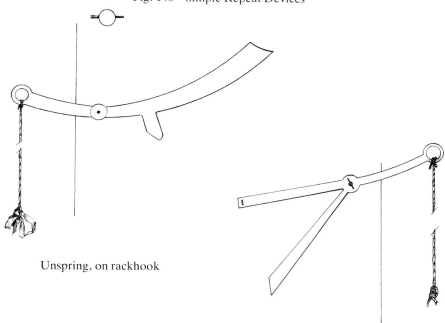

Unspring, on rackhook

Unsprung, on lifting/warning piece

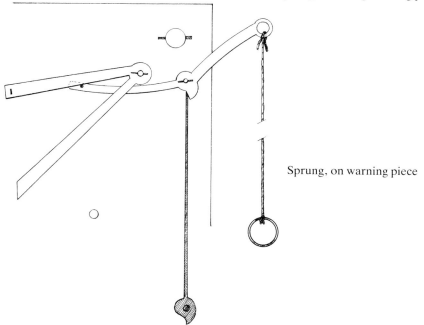

Sprung, on warning piece

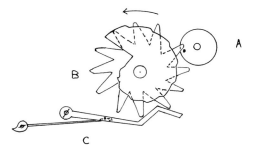

Jumper starwheel for repeatwork

A   Cannon pinion with operating pin
B   Starwheel attached below reversed snail
C   Jumper and jumper spring

set it up carefully with the locking-piece against the locking pin when the hammer tail is clear of hammer pins, and you will have to lift the front plate to adjust things if this is not achieved.

Repeat Striking

Striking can be repeated (by pulling a cord) only with the rack system; if you try to repeat with the countwheel mechanism, you let off the next hour's strike. This may be desirable for adjustment, so there may be what looks like a 'repeat' hook to pull. Rack striking was designed precisely for its 'repeat' facility, and this was much exploited for bracket clocks. Rack striking was almost universal in eight-day clocks and many longcase clocks were originally made to repeat. Most of them date from the eighteenth century. It seems that rack striking was used as a domestic signal, like a dinner-gong, although the survival of a few clocks able to pull-repeat quarter-striking suggests that even with longcase clocks it was partly for use at night, and occasionally there are traces of pulley-systems leading off to an upper room. Nowadays most repeat devices have long been removed, but they are recognizable by remaining springs and screw-holes.

The commonest device for hour repeat in longcase clocks is shown in Fig. 146. At the top right of the frontplate (though left-hand working is also met) is a pivoted lever having at its inner end a hook to raise the warning-piece, and with the outer end extended to take the knot or loop of a pull-cord. A stout blade spring was often arranged to hold the inner end down until the cord was pulled. When repeating was on the left hand side it might be contrived by an extension of the rack-hook.

This mechanism is simple enough and presents no problems in working or, indeed, in restoration, should it be missing. In use, however, the effect does tend to depend on how the cord is pulled, since the rack has to be fully released. More sophisticated arrangements, involving a separate repeat train, are outside this book's scope.

Longcase repeat devices normally have only a simple snail to control the striking, and so are capable of error up to an hour. Sometimes a more sensitive arrangement was used in smaller repeating clocks. Here the snail does not move continuously but is 'jumped' forward immediately before the hour, reducing the margin for error, by a pin on the cannon pinion (see Fig. 146).

Appendix

Preparation of Glue and Polish

1. Preparing Scotch Glue

To prepare Scotch glue for use, either use a proprietary double glue pot or half fill a small tin with glue pearls, and immerse in a larger tin full of water, just cover with cold water, and stir every few minutes. It is not necessary to leave pearls soaking for twenty-four hours – this simply delays liquefying when heat is applied. After twenty minutes it should look like brown tapioca pudding or frogspawn!

Have a larger tin one-third full of water, place the small tin inside (making sure that it cannot fall over) and heat very gently on a stove or electric ring. The water in the large tin should be just steaming, never boiling. Gradually your Scotch glue will turn liquid with a slight skin on top. This will take three-quarters of an hour or so. You can tell if the glue is the right temperature for use by just dabbing a tiny bit on the back of your hand. If it hurts, it's hot enough! The consistency of the glue is also important. It is at the right thickness if, when you hold the brush up, the glue flows off steadily without appearing lumpy, and without the flow breaking up into little droplets. If it is too lumpy, add a little hot water, stir it in and try again in a little while. If the flow breaks up into droplets, the glue is too thin. Do not add more pearls (unless you kept back some of the soaked ones) but just leave the glue for a little while longer, when some of the water will evaporate.

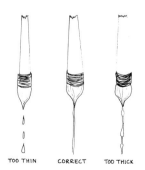

TOO THIN   CORRECT   TOO THICK

Fig. 147   Assessing Scotch glue thickness

Scotch glue will stay at the right temperature in the gluepot for up to an hour once liquid, and can be reheated once or twice if it has cooled off overnight (though you may need to add more water).

2. *Preparing Polishing Wax*

To make your own wax polish, melt together, in a double boiler, equal weights of carnauba wax and beeswax. Break them into small pieces if necessary to speed up the melting. Ensure that the tin in which you are mixing them is only one-third to one-half full – you will need the extra space when actually using the polish. Apply moderate heat. When both waxes are completely mixed, add one or two capfuls of pure turpentine. Mix well, then remove from the heat and allow to cool and set. The polish may take as long as a couple of days to set right through. It is then ready for use as described in Chapter 17.

3. *Preparing Stopping Wax*

To make your own stopping wax, melt together, in a double boiler, nine parts of beeswax to one part of carnauba wax (by weight). Add pigment for the colour you require. When it is warm, you can cast the wax into moulds which are easy for handling – the fingers of a rubber glove are very effective – or you can use tinfoil to make button-shaped moulds since this wax, unlike polish which is applied with a cloth, is rubbed directly into the wood.

List of Suppliers

The following suppliers are among those offering mail order services:

Clock Parts and Tools

Apollo-Southerns Watch and Clock Supplies, Tonypandy, South Wales CF40 1JA

Hadfield, G.K., Beck Bank, Great Salkeld, Penrith, Cumbria CA11 9LN

Meadows and Passmore, 1 Ellen Street, Portslade, Brighton, East Sussex BN41 1EU

Richards of Burton, Woodhouse Clock Works, Swadlincote Road, Woodville, Burton-on-Trent DE11 8DA

Rose, R.E., 731 Sidcup Road, Eltham, London SE9 3SA

H.S. Walsh & Sons Ltd, 243 Beckenham Road, Beckenham, Kent BR3 4TS

Old Movements and Parts

Olivers, 15 Cross Street, Hove, E. Sussex BN3 1AJ.

Clock Case Materials, Polishing and Finishing Supplies

Richard Barry Southern Marketing Ltd, Unit 1, 2 Chapel Place, Portslade, Brighton, East Sussex BN41 1DR

Restoration Materials, Proctor Street, Bury, Lancashire BL8 2NY

The Tool Post, 35 Brunstock Beck, Didcot, Oxfordshire OX11 7YG

Veneers

Art Veneers Co. Ltd, Chiswick Avenue, Industrial Estate, Mildenhall, Suffolk IP28 7AY

J. Crispin, 92–96 Curtain Row, London EC2A 3AA

Locks, Hinges, etc.

Classic Brass, Classic House, 1 West Road, Westcliff-on-Sea, Essex SS90
   9DD

Select Further Reading

Historical and Reference

Baillie, G.H. & Loomes, B., *Watchmakers and Clockmakers of the World* (NAG Press, Vol I, 1929, and Vol II, B. Loomes, 1986)

Brown, C. & M., *The Clockmakers of Llanrwst* (Bridge Books, Wrexham 1993)

Bruton, E., *The Longcase Clock* (Hart-Davis, 1970)

Cescinsky, H. & Webster, M.R., *English Domestic Clocks* (Hamlyn, 1918)

Loomes, B., *Antique British Clocks* (Hale, 1991)

Loomes, B., *Grandfather Clocks and their Cases* (David & Charles, 1985)

Peate, Iorwell C., *Clock and Watch Makers in Wales* (1960)

Roberts, D., *British Longcase Clocks* (Schiffer, Pennsylvania, 1990)

Robinson, T., *The Longcase Clock* (Antique Collectors Club, 1981)

Smith, John, *Old Scottish Clockmakers* (1921)

Practical

Bennet, M., *Restoring Antique Furniture* (Cassell, 1990)

De Carle, D., *Practical Clock Repairing* (NAG, 1952)

Gazeley, W.J., *Watch and Clock Making and Reparing* (Hale, 1993)

Joyce, E., *The Technique of Furniture Making* (Batsford, 1970)

Penman, L., *The Clock-Repairer's Handbook* (David and Charles, 1985)

Smith, E., *Clocks and Clock-Repairing* (Lutterworth, 1979)

——, *Repairing Antique Clocks* (David & Charles, 1973)

——, *Striking and Chiming Clocks* (David & Charles, 1985)

Taylor, V.J., *The Construction of Period Country Furniture* (Stobart Davies, 1978)

Taylor, V.J. and Babb, H.A., *Making and Repairing Wooden Clock Cases* (David & Charles, 1986)

Tyler, E.J., *Clock Types* (Longmans, 1982)

Walker, A., *The Encyclopaedia of Wood* (Facts on File, 1989)

Wilding, J., *How to Repair Antique Clocks* (Meridian Clocks, Lurgashall, East Sussex GU28 9EW)

Magazines

Horological Journal – British Horological Institute, Newark, Notts NG23 5TE

Antiquarian Horology – High Street, Ticehurst, Wadhurst, East Sussex TN5 7AL

The Antique Dealer and Collector's Guide – IPC Magazines Ltd.

Clocks – Nexus Media Ltd, Nexus House, Boundary Way, Hemel Hempstead HP2 7ST

Furniture – Guild of Master-Craftsmen Publications, Castle Place, 166 High Street, Lewes BN7 1XU

Specialist Booksellers (Horological)

G.K. Hadfield, Beck Bank, Great Salkeld, Penrith, Cumbria CA11 9LN

Rita Shenton, 148 Percy Road, Twickenham TW2 6JG

Index